THE IROQUOIS CONFEDERACY

HISTORY AND LEGENDS

Emerson Klees

Cameo Press, Rochester, New York

Imprint of Friends of the Finger Lakes Publishing

Other books about New York State by Emerson Klees

Persons, Places, and Things In the Finger Lakes Region
    (1993, 2000)
Person, Places, and Things Around the Finger Lakes Region
    (1994)
People of the Finger Lakes Region (1995)
Legends and Stories of the Finger Lakes Region (1995)
The Erie Canal In the Finger Lakes Region (1996)
Underground Railroad Tales With Routes Through the
    Finger Lakes Region (1997, 2002)
More Legends and Stories of the Finger Lakes Region (1997)
The Women's Rights Movement and the Finger Lakes Region
    (1998)
Wineries of the Finger Lakes Region (2000, 2003)
The Crucible of Ferment: New York's Psychic Highway (2001)

Friends of the Finger Lakes Publishing
P. O. Box 18131
Rochester, New York 14618

Library of Congress Control Number: 2003092506

ISBN 1-891046-04-7

Printed in the United States of America
9 8 7 6 5 4 3 2 1

PREFACE

"Great Spirit, grant that I may not criticize my neighbor until I have walked a mile in his moccasins."

Joshua V. H. Clark, "Indian Prayer"

Iroquois Confederacy: History and Legends provides an overview of the migration of Native Americans to the Northeast and the events that impacted the Iroquois Confederacy, along with a brief history of the six nations of the Confederacy: Senecas, Cayugas, Onondagas, Tuscaroras, Oneidas, and Mohawks. Thirty legends, grouped by nation, are provided as well as six "origin" legends and 10 "selected" legends about the Confederacy.

Nine personalities are profiled:
- Joseph Brant
- Handsome Lake
- Hiawatha
- Mary Jemison
- Chief Logan
- Lewis Henry Morgan, "Grand Tekarihogea"
- Ely Parker
- Red Jacket
- Kateri Tekakwitha

For example, Ely Parker was a Seneca chief, a lawyer, an engineer, and a brigadier general on General Grant's staff who transcribed the surrender agreement between Generals Grant and Lee to conclude the Civil War. Kateri Tekakwitha, a Mohawk maiden who died at the age of 24, has been beatified by the Catholic Church and is progressing toward canonization.

The book contains a chapter on Iroquois culture, including highlights of the matrilineal society of the Iroquois and of life in the longhouse. The epilogue provides an overview of the Six Nations of the Confederacy in the 20th and 21st centuries with a section on the "high-steel" Mohawks who helped to build skyscrapers and bridges in the United States and Canada.

The goal of the book is to provide an understanding of those who were here before us and, until they were dispersed by General Sullivan's campaign during the Revolutionary War, were one of the most advanced Indian cultures in North America. Many of the legends are reprinted from *Legends and Stories of the Finger Lakes Region* and *More Legends and Stories of the Finger Lakes Region*.

LIST OF PHOTOGRAPHS

Cover: "Sky Woman" by Ernest Smith, Courtesy Rochester Museum &
Science Center Indian Arts Project Collection

Page No.

Cover design by Dunn and Rice Design, Inc., Rochester, NY
Maps by Actionmaps, Rochester, NY

TABLE OF CONTENTS

Page No.

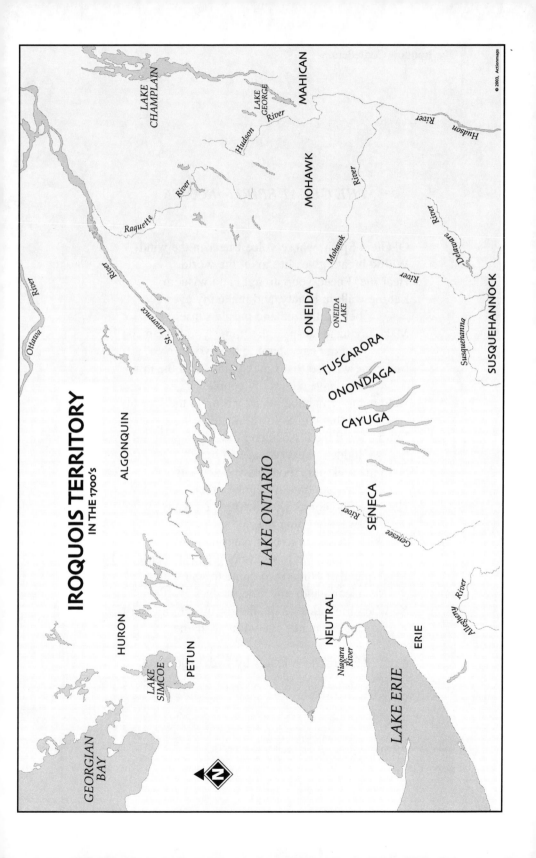

IROQUOIS TERRITORY
IN THE 1700's

GEORGIAN BAY

LAKE SIMCOE

HURON

PETUN

ALGONQUIN

NEUTRAL

Niagara River

LAKE ERIE

ERIE

Allegheny River

SENECA

Genesee River

CAYUGA

ONONDAGA

TUSCARORA

SENECA

LAKE ONTARIO

St. Lawrence

River

Ottawa River

Raquette River

River

LAKE CHAMPLAIN

LAKE GEORGE

MAHICAN

Hudson River

MOHAWK

Mohawk River

River

ONEIDA

ONEIDA LAKE

Delaware River

Susquehanna

River

SUSQUEHANNOCK

Hudson River

© 2003, Actionmaps

THE GREAT SPIRIT PRAYER

O' Great Spirit, whose voice I hear in the wind,
Whose breath gives life to all the world.
Hear me; I need your strength and wisdom.
Let me walk in beauty, and make my eyes ever
       behold the red and purple sunset.
Make my hands respect the things you have made
       and my ears sharp to hear your voice.
Make me wise so that I may understand the things
       you have taught my people.
Help me to remain calm and strong in the face of
       all that comes towards me.
Let me learn the lessons you have
       hidden in every leaf and rock.
Help me seek pure thoughts and act with
       the intention of helping others.
Help me find compassion without empathy
       overwhelming me.
I seek strength, not to be greater than my
       brother, but to fight my greatest enemy—Myself.
Make me always ready to come to you with
       clean hands and straight eyes.
So when life fades, as the fading sunset, my spirit
       may come to you without shame.

From *The Iroquois* by Lydia Bjornland

Statue of Chief Montour, Painted Post

PROLOGUE

MIGRATION OF NATIVE AMERICANS TO THE NORTHEASTERN UNITED STATES

"The Iroquois in their best days were the noblest and most interesting of all Indians who have lived on this continent north of Mexico. They were truly the men whose Indian name signifies: 'We surpass all others.' They alone founded a political institution and gained political supremacy. With European civilization still unknown to them, they had given birth to self-government in America. They founded independence, erected a union of states, carried their arms far beyond their borders, and made their conquests permanent. The conquered people becoming tributary states much after the manner of those which Rome conquered two thousand years before them. In diplomacy, the Iroquois matched the White man from Europe. They had self-control, knowledge of human nature, tact, and sagacity, and they often became arbitrators between other people."

J. K. Bloomfield, *The Oneidas*

Origin of the Iroquois

Speculation about the ancestry of the Indians in the northeastern United States has occurred for centuries. No evidence of *Homo Erectus,* predecessor of *Homo Sapiens*, has been found in the Western Hemisphere. Scientists conjecture that the forefathers of the North American Indians either migrated here intentionally or were on boats that were blown off course. Speculators about the Indians' ancestors include those who consider them descendants of the ten lost tribes of Israel. *The Book of Mormon* of the Church of Jesus Christ of Latter-Day Saints relates that the Indians descended from the Lamanites, an element of the Jewish ethnic group.

However, the consensus of scientific opinion is that ancestors of the Indians migrated from Asia across the present-day Bering Strait about 12,000 to 15,000 years ago. The formation of the Wisconsin glacial drift during the Pleistocene Epoch Ice Age caused the water level in the oceans to drop from 150 to 300 feet. A land bridge that measured 1,000-feet wide emerged between the Chuckchi Peninsula of Siberia and the Seward Peninsula of Alaska, which today are separated by the 56-mile-wide Bering Strait.

The Indians' ancestors probably migrated across the land bridge in search of food. Among the animals that migrated from Asia were the forerunners of the bison, camel, horse, mammoth, mastodon, opossum, sloth, weasel, and wild dog. Camels, mammoths, mastodons, and sloths subsequently died out here.

Prehistoric hunters from times up to about 7,000 years ago are called Paleo-Indians. Tools for hunting and food preparation were developed from 8,500 to 13,000 years ago. The spear was the principal weapon, and many large spear points have been found from that era. Men hunted large animals, and women fished, gathered wild plants, and snared small animals. Women were the main providers of food in the hunter-gatherer culture.

Ancestors of the American Indians migrated southward from Alaska and Canada to the western United States. Spear points have been found in many sites, including major finds in New Mexico at Clovis, Folsom, and the Sandia Mountains. Migration continued eastward to the midwestern and eastern United States and southward through Central America to South America.

Between 8500 and 6500 BC, Ice Age mammals such as mammoths and mastodons became extinct. The Paleo-Indian Stage ended along with the hunting of big game, and the Archaic Stage began. The grinding and polishing of stone artifacts and the making of pottery began in the Archaic Stage. Sources of food were birds, deer, fish, shellfish, and wild plants. Making artifacts from copper reached its peak in the western Great Lakes Region from 3,000 to 4,000 years ago.

Agriculture began in North America about 7,000 years ago, which was about the time that small ears of wild maize were cultivated. Cultivation of beans began about 6,000 years ago. About 3,500 years ago, the Archaic Stage was marked by two developments: the use of pottery and an increase in burial observances. The Woodland Culture during this period was typified by the building of mounds in which eminent people and accompanying funeral offerings were buried.

Indians of the Woodland Period
The culture of the Owasco Indians of the late Woodland Period that spanned the years AD 1000-1300 was determined by carbon dating of hearth charcoal samples from eight separate sites. The Owascos were farmers, fisherman, and hunters. They grew herbs and tobacco and were the earliest culture in New York State known to grow beans, corn, and squash. The Owasco people made items such as bone awls and needles, clay storage and cooking pots, flint projectile points, stone ax heads and scraping tools, and wooden bowls and spoons.

In 1915, E. H. Gohl discovered pottery and other Indian artifacts on the site of the 12th-century Owasco Indian village in present-day Emerson Park, south of Auburn. The site was excavated later that year by Dr. Arthur C. Parker, New York State Archaeologist and Director Emeritus of the Rochester Museum & Science Center. It was the first excavation in the region to yield pre-Iroquois artifacts. Because of many later excavations, the Owasco culture is the best-known pre-Iroquois culture in New York State. The culture was named "Owasco" because of its proximity to Owasco Lake.

Many bone, stone, and ceramic objects, including pipes and large pots produced by the Owascos, were excavated. Most of the material found on the site is now in the New York State Museum in Albany.

The Archaic Stage

The Archaic Stage in the northeastern United States had four cultures: Lamoka, Frontenac, Laurentian I, and Laurentian II. The Lamoka culture began about 3500 BC. The Lamokas were hunters, fishermen, and gatherers of wild plants. Their main weapons were the spear and spear-thrower. They used beveled stone adzes in woodworking. The Lamoka culture overlapped the time of the Frontenac and Laurentian I cultures; similarities exist among all three cultures.

People of the Lamoka culture lived in central New York until after 2000 BC. Lamoka people moved into the region because of the ample supply of fish and game. In 1925, one of the earliest and largest excavations yielding information about their culture was dug near Lamoka Lake in the town of Tyrone in Schuyler County. Lamoka Lake and its companion, Waneta Lake, straddle the county road between Hammondsport and Watkins Glen. Waneta Lake, north of the road, is joined to Lamoka Lake, south of the road, by a three-quarter-mile-long channel that is navigable by small boats.

The 1925 excavation site is at the head of Lamoka Lake and is only several feet above the level of the channel that connects the lakes. Subsequent excavations were made at the site in 1958 and 1962. Many antler, bone, and stone artifacts were found that were helpful in defining Lamoka culture. The stone artifacts included anvils, beveled adzes, hammerstones, and projectile points.

The Lamokas depended upon hunting, fishing, and gathering wild plants for their subsistence. They were not farmers like the Owasco and the Iroquois that would populate the region many years later. The Lamoka's principal foods were deer, passenger pigeon, and turkey. The spear was their main weapon; they also used snares and traps. The fish upon which they subsisted included bullheads and pickerel. Acorns were an important source of food. Many implements were found that they used to grind acorns into flour.

The typical Lamoka adult male was of medium height (five feet, five inches to five feet, six inches tall), had a slender build, and had a long, narrow, oval-shaped head with a narrow nose. The social organization of the Lamokas was comprised of groups of nuclear and extended families bound by common needs, such as food gathering and defense.

A nominal chief who served in an advisory capacity was probably the only central authority. Eventually, the Lamoka culture was assimilated into other cultures and ceased to exist as a separate culture after 2000 BC.

People of the Frontenac Culture obtained food by hunting, fishing, and gathering wild plants. The dog, which they revered, was their only domestic animal. The Laurentian I people were also hunters, fishermen, and gatherers. They located their villages along rivers. The Laurentian II people lived at a later time than the Laurentian I Culture but obtained their food from the same sources. The Laurentian II people were the first group of Archaic people in central New York to create pottery, which was crude in nature, and ground-slate tools.

Mound-builder / Owasco Cultures
The Hopewell people, named for a farm-owner in Ross County, Ohio, operated on a grander scale than their predecessors. They built larger mounds with richer burial offerings because of their extensive trade with surrounding people. They flourished from about 400 BC until AD 500. They are also known as Mound-builders. New York Hopewell people migrated from the Midwest at a later time, probably from AD 1100 to 1300.

The Owasco culture of the Late Prehistoric Period existed from about AD 1300 to 1600. The Owascos obtained most of their food from farming, particularly the cultivation of corn and beans. They supplemented their food supply by fishing and hunting. Their villages were built near lakes and streams and were surrounded by wooden stockades. Their pottery was superior to the crude pottery of the Archaic Period.

The Iroquois Confederacy
Ancestors of the Iroquois nations moved into New York State from the Great Lakes Region and from the St. Lawrence River Region. According to Indian legend, the origin of the Iroquois Confederacy occurred in 1570, when a prophet, Deganawida, ended warfare among the nations of the Confederacy and established the "Great Peace."

Deganawida had a dream of an evergreen tree extending through the sky to the land of the Great Spirit. The tree was the tree of sisterhood, not of brotherhood; the Iroquois were a matrilineal society. The five roots of the tree represented the original nations of the Iroquois Confederacy: Senecas, Cayugas, Onondagas, Oneidas, and Mohawks.

Deganawida's dream was brought to fruition by Hiawatha, who traveled from nation to nation advocating peace. In 1722, the Tuscaroras, who had migrated northward from North Carolina, became the sixth nation of the Iroquois Confederacy. Later, the Delawares came under the protection of the Iroquois, south of the Finger Lakes Region.

The Iroquois Confederacy had 50 sachems, or League chiefs, i.e. members of the governing body: the Onondagas had 14, the Cayugas had 10, the Mohawks and Oneidas had nine each, and the Senecas (the largest nation) had eight. All decisions reached by the council of sachems had to be unanimous.

On July 8, 1788, the Iroquois Confederacy signed a treaty that conveyed 2,600,000 acres of land to the Phelps and Gorham Company for $5,000 and an annuity of $500. The Phelps-Gorham Purchase extended from the Pennsylvania border along a line near Geneva to Sodus Bay on Lake Ontario in the east, and to the Genesee River in the west—including a small parcel of land west of the Genesee River bordering on Lake Ontario.

Cherry Valley Monument, Cherry Valley

INTRODUCTION

EVENTS THAT IMPACTED THE IROQUOIS CONFEDERACY

"Their [the Iroquois Confederacy's] government was the most integrated and orderly north of Mexico, and some have thought it gave suggestions to the American Constitution ([Richard Henry] Lee, Franklin, Jefferson, and Washington were quite familiar with the League). They developed what came close to an empire, with conquered nations paying tribute and taking their orders. For over a hundred years, they held a pivotal position between the French and the English. It seems very possible that, except for the Iroquois, North America at this day might have been French."

Ruth M. Underhill, *Red Man's America*

The French Expedition to the Finger Lakes Region

In June 1687, Marquis de Nonville, Governor of New France, assembled a military expedition comprised of 2,000 French Army regulars and 600 Indian allies. The expedition traveled down the St. Lawrence River and across Lake Ontario to Irondequoit Bay, east of present-day Rochester, in 200 bateaux and 200 canoes. Another force of 180 Frenchmen and over 300 Indians, commanded by La Durantaye and Tonty, met the larger force at Irondequoit Bay. De Nonville left 300 men to build a small fort to protect the barges and canoes and then marched overland to attack the Senecas. His goal was to reduce his competition in the fur trade.

De Nonville followed the Great Indian Trail to Ganondagan, south of today's village of Victor. As he approached the major Seneca village through a ravine on July 13, 1687, his expedition was surprised by a Seneca ambush and was almost overwhelmed. Some of his Indian allies fled, but his Mohawk allies held. De Nonville ordered the sounding of trumpets and the roll of drums while executing a flanking movement to rout the Senecas. Over 100 Frenchmen and 80 Senecas were killed. In retreating, the Senecas burned their village but not their store of corn. The French invaders tore down the Senecas' palisades and completed the destruction.

De Nonville's men burned three other Seneca villages and destroyed their stored corn and beans. His expedition then marched to their boats at Irondequoit Bay and returned to Canada. No lasting benefit came to the French from this military venture. Ganondagan was not rebuilt; the Senecas merely moved farther inland, away from Lake Ontario. The action drove the Senecas into alliances with the British that continued through the Revolutionary War.

The Wyoming Massacre

The 25-mile-long Wyoming Valley is part of the Susquehanna River Valley north of Wilkes-Barre, Pennsylvania. The Shawnees were driven out of the valley by the Delawares, who were in turn evicted by the Iroquois. In Colonial times, both Connecticut and Pennsylvania claimed the region due to misinterpretation of Royal grants. Pioneers from these two colonies fought each other for several years. The last battle occurred in 1775, when Connecticut militia defeated the Pennsylvanians.

Early in the Revolutionary War, the valley was occupied by about 4,000 pioneers from Connecticut. The closest White settlement, inhabited by Pennsylvanians, was 60 miles away. The Connecticut pioneers were disliked by both the Delawares and the Iroquois. The Wyoming Valley prospered, and the region provided large quantities of wheat to General Washington's army. The area sent two companies of soldiers to the Continental Army, which considerably reduced the number of able-bodied men in the valley.

In June 1778, the British increased their military operations against the frontier. Wyoming, known to be vulnerable to attack, was chosen as their first target. The British planned to use the valley as a base for attacking the Mohawk Valley to the north. Colonel John Butler advanced from Niagara to Tioga with 300 Rangers, Royal Greens and Tories. This contingent was joined by 800 Senecas lead by Chief Kayingwaurto ("Old King").

On July 2, 1778, this force of 1,100 men traveled by canoe from Tioga to a point just north of the Wyoming settlement. Fort Wintermoot, commanded by Lieutenant Elisha Scoville, was the first Colonial fort that they encountered. Most of Scoville's militiamen were Tories; they forced him to open the fort's gate to the advancing British and their Seneca allies. The poorly constructed Fort Jenkins, a mile south of Fort Wintermoot, was defended by only 20 men who fell to the British after a short fight.

Next came Fort Wyoming, also called Forty Fort, commanded by Colonel Zebulon Butler with a force of 60 Colonial troops and 300 militia. Colonel Dennison was second-in-command. Zebulon Butler knew that his force should stay in the fort, but his militia did not want to see their homes destroyed. They prevailed upon him to mount a surprise attack on the advancing British. His 360 men fought valiantly but were overwhelmed by British Colonel John Butler's force.

The Seneca allies of the British went around the Colonials by wading through a swamp to attack their rear. Colonel Zebulon Butler ordered the right wing of his force to fall back to fight the Senecas behind them. Unfortunately, his command was misunderstood as a call for a general retreat. The battle turned into a rout; only 60 Americans reached the fort. Colonel John Butler, in demanding its surrender, offered to spare the soldiers' lives except for Colonel Zebulon Butler. He and his Colonials escaped, leaving

Colonel Dennison to surrender the fort.

Colonel John Butler restrained his men, and only Colonial men under arms were killed. Civilian men, women, and children fled to the swamps on their way to the nearest settlement, 60 miles away. Butler's Seneca allies burned down every house in the settlement. Butler and his Tories returned to Niagara, and the Senecas went back to their longhouses. A regiment of Colonial troops was detailed to protect the rebuilt Fort Wyoming from attack.

The Cherry Valley Massacre

In the autumn of 1778, Walter Butler, Colonel John Butler's son, was commissioned captain in Butler's Rangers. Captain Butler and a contingent of Rangers traveled to Chemung, where he made his headquarters. He was joined there by Mohawk Chief Joseph Brant and a large party of Iroquois. Captain Butler, second-in-command to his father, was in charge of the combined forces.

British plans to invade the Mohawk Valley and the Schoharie Valley from the south were stymied by the Colonial Fort Alden at Cherry Valley. If Butler could destroy it, the Mohawk Valley west of Schenectady would be vulnerable. Colonel Ichabod Alden, the stubborn, strong-willed commander of the fort, had been warned that Butler and Brant were assembling a force on the Susquehanna River with plans to attack Fort Alden. General Hand, Colonial commander at Albany, was advised of this threat by the Oneidas and asked Colonel Klock to dispatch 200 men to reinforce the fort.

Residents of Cherry Valley, frightened by this threat, asked Colonel Alden if they could stay in the fort. He denied their request, telling them that it was an empty threat and that the Indians would not attack this late in the season. To display his confidence to the residents, Colonel Alden and most of his staff slept the night of November 10 in private homes away from the fort. Alden sent a scouting party of nine men down the valley.

That day, Butler's force of 50 British regulars, 150 Tories, and 600 Iroquois came up the valley. Most of the Iroquois were Mohawks commanded by Brant and Senecas under Chief Hiakatoo ("Little Beard"). They found Alden's nine scouts sleeping around a campfire and captured them. The attacking force slept in rain and snow that night and attacked the next morning.

Colonel Alden and Lieutenant Stacy spent that night a quarter of a mile from the fort at the home of Mr. Wells, an acquaintance of Butler and Brant. Both knew from captured scouts that Alden had only a small guard with him. The Iroquois attacked the Wells home while Butler advanced on the fort. Colonel Alden was tomahawked and scalped while running to the fort, and Lieutenant Stacy was captured. All Colonials outside of the fort were either killed or captured.

Men in the fort barely had time to close the gates before the attackers arrived. Butler persisted with his advance on the fort but was unable to capture it. His Indian allies, who did not favor attacks on fortified sites, became impatient. The Senecas of Chief Hiakatoo were smarting from their losses at Oriskany, and Chief Brant's Mohawks sought revenge for the destruction of their villages at Oquaga and Unadilla and their longhouses and food storage sites along the Susquehanna and Unadilla Rivers.

The Iroquois did not want to wait for the main army to capture the fort. They systematically collected scalps, including those of women and children. Captain Butler became aware of this, but before he could send Captain McDonald and a detachment of Rangers to stop it, 31 civilians in seven homes had been killed. Some civilians escaped to the woods; Captain McDonald protected the rest for the duration of the battle. When Butler stopped the attack, he took 40 men and 135 women and children prisoners.

An attack on the fort the next day was also unsuccessful. Brant released all but two women and nine children before returning to Niagara. These prisoners were retained as exchanges for Captain Butler's mother and eight of her friends being held by General Philip Schuyler. Women and children were well treated as prisoners of both British and Colonial armies.

Although Butler did not capture Fort Alden, the results of his campaign could have been worse. Over 3,000 Colonial regulars and militia were within three days' march of Fort Alden, and Colonel Klock's 200 men sent to reinforce the garrison at the fort arrived a day late. Captain Butler's reputation suffered considerably because of the atrocities committed by his Iroquois allies. Nevertheless, he acted to protect the civilians as soon as he heard of their fate.

The Sullivan Campaign

In 1778, massacre of White settlers by Indians at Wyoming (Wilkes-Barre), Pennsylvania, and Cherry Valley, New York, caused considerable anxiety among pioneers in the region. The British tried to convince their Indian allies, four of the six nations of the Iroquois Confederacy, to attack General Washington's Colonial Army from the west. On February 27, 1779, Congress authorized General Washington to form an expedition to remove this threat.

Washington offered command of the expedition to 39-year-old Major General John Sullivan, who had distinguished himself in the battles of Brandywine, Germantown, Trenton, and Princeton, and particularly in leading the bayonet charge at Butt's Hill. Sullivan's army assembled at Easton, Pennsylvania, stopped at Wyoming, Pennsylvania, to correct supply problems, and marched to Tioga Point (now Athens), Pennsylvania.

Another component of the expedition started from Schenectady, commanded by Brigadier General James Clinton, Sullivan's second-in-command. Clinton's men built 212 boats and moved up the Mohawk River to Canajoharie where they carried the boats overland to Otsego Lake. They built a dam at Cooperstown, raised the level of Otsego Lake by two feet, and proceeded southward to meet Sullivan at Tioga Point. Sullivan's men built Fort Sullivan at Tioga Point and waited for Clinton's forces to arrive.

General Clinton arrived in late August, and both elements of the expedition marched to Newtown, five miles south of Elmira. They were met by a force of 1,100 Tories, Canadian Rangers, and Indians. The force opposing Sullivan was commanded by Mohawk Chief Joseph Brant. Brant had been educated by Eleazar Wheelock, who subsequently founded Dartmouth College. Sullivan's army of over 3,000 routed Brant's force, partly because the Colonials worked in behind Brant's men and waited in ambush in the only staged battle of the campaign.

Sullivan's expedition caused considerable destruction of Indian villages, crops, storehouses, and orchards in the Finger Lakes Region, particularly around Cayuga and Seneca Lakes. Of the six major lakes, Keuka Lake was the only one not visited by Sullivan's men. His army traveled as far west as the Genesee River; it marched by the northern ends of Canandaigua, Honeoye, and

Hemlock Lakes and the southern end of Conesus Lake.

On the expedition's return from the western part of the region, Colonel Peter Gansevoort was sent to Albany with a detachment of 100 men who passed through the sites of Auburn and Skaneateles. At the close of the expedition, Sullivan reported that he had destroyed 40 Iroquois villages, 160,000 bushels of corn, large quantities of other crops, and many acres of orchards.

Sullivan had complied with Washington's order: "It is proposed to carry the war into the heart of the country of the Six Nations, to cut off their settlements, destroy their next year's crops ... lay waste all the settlements around, so that the country may not only be over-run but destroyed." General Sullivan had accomplished the goals of removing the British threat from the West and of preventing the Six Nations from making war as a confederacy. Unfortunately, he had also destroyed one of the most advanced Native-American cultures until that time.

* * *

CLANS OF THE IROQUOIS CONFEDERACY

Seneca	Cayuga	Onondaga	Tuscarora	Oneida	Mohawk
Turtle	Turtle	Turtle	Turtle	Turtle	Turtle
Bear		Bear	Bear	Bear	Bear
Wolf	Wolf	Wolf	Wolf	Wolf	Wolf
Snipe	Snipe	Snipe	Snipe		
Hawk		Hawk			
	Deer	Deer	Deer		
		Beaver	Beaver		
		Eel	Eel		

A clan is an element of Native-American society that traces its descent from a common ancestor. Membership in a clan is the basis for membership in a tribe. Because the Iroquois have a matrilineal society, descent is traced through the mother's line. Clans are divided into moieties, or sides.

POPULATION OF THE IROQUOIS CONFEDERACY 1630-1770

Year	Seneca	Cayuga	Onondaga	Oneida	Mohawk	Total
1630	4,000	4,000	4,000	2,000	7,740	21,740
1640	4,000	2,000	2,000	1,000	2,835	11,835
1650	4,000	1,200	1,200	600	1,734	8,734
1660	4,000	1,200	1,200	400	2,304	9,184
1670	4,000	1,200	1,300	600	1,985	9,085
1680	4,000	1,200	1,400	800	1,000	8,400
1690	4,000	1,280	2,000	720	1,000	8,920
1700	2,400	800	1,000	280	620	5,100
1710	4,000	600	1,400	480	620	7,100
1720	2,800	520	1,000	800	580	5,700
1730	1,400	480	800	400	580	3,660
1740	2,000	500	800	400	580	4,280
1750	2,000	500	800	800	580	4,680
1760	4,200	504	544	1,000	640	6,888
1770	4,000	1,040	800	800	640	7,280

From *The Iroquois Source* by Dean R. Snow. Excludes Tuscaroras who joined the Iroquois Confederacy in 1722. In 1713, 500 Tuscarora families moved from North Carolina to live among the Iroquois. Another 160 Tuscaroras moved north to live on land provided by the Oneidas in 1766.

Seneca Iroquois National Museum, Salamanca

CHAPTER 1

THE SENECA NATION

"Of these [Iroquois] Nations, the Seneca people are usually considered the most highly developed.... They occupied the whole western half of what is today the State of New York, and there is a theory that their exceptional qualities were stimulated by their peculiar position between the western non-Iroquois Indians, against whom they had to stand as a bulwark and who kept them alert and resourceful, and the rest of their people to the east of them, who protected them from the pressures of the English and Dutch."

Edmund Wilson, *Apologies to the Iroquois*

HISTORY

The Seneca Nation, "Keepers of the Western Door," were the largest of the Iroquois Nations but had the fewest chiefs (eight) on the Council of the Confederacy. The Senecas lived between the Genesee River and Canandaigua Lake in what are now Livingston, Ontario, and (southern) Monroe Counties in New York State.

Seneca hunting grounds initially extended from Lake Ontario southward to the inlets of Conesus, Hemlock, Canadice, and Honeoye Lakes and eastward to the "between-the-lakes" area separating Seneca and Cayuga Lakes. After successful campaigns against the Eries, Neutrals, and Hurons, Senecas expanded their hunting grounds west of the Genesee River into Ohio and northward into Ontario, Canada.

During the first half of the 16th century, the Seneca Nation had two major villages, a western and an eastern, and two smaller villages near each other, north of Hemlock Lake. As the land around the villages was cleared of firewood, the Senecas moved every 10 to 20 years.

Seventeenth Century

Senecas of the western village moved northward along Spring Brook to Honeoye Creek. Those who lived in the eastern village initially moved northeasterly to Honeoye Creek and then to tributaries of Ganargua Creek.

Senecas were heavily involved in the fur trade, even though they were the farthest Iroquois nation from Dutch traders in the Hudson Valley and from French traders along the St. Lawrence River. However, they were closest to the expanding beaver trapping grounds in the west toward Ohio.

In 1649, Senecas and Mohawks burned the Huron villages of St. Ignace and St. Louis in Canada and then attacked the Neutrals and the Petuns, allies of the Hurons. In 1653, the Iroquois sent a delegation to Montreal to make peace with the French. The following year, at a council with Father Simon Le Moyne at Onondaga, Senecas expressed their support for this peace, which unfortunately did not last long.

In 1656, Jesuit priest Pierre Joseph Marie Chaumonot visited the Seneca villages and reported that the main Seneca village, the capital, was at Ganondagan, south of the present village of Victor. In 1668, Jesuits established a permanent mission among the Senecas. In 1687, when de Nonville raided the palisaded village of Ganondagan, he reported that the Seneca Nation still had two major villages, each with over 100 longhouses, and two smaller villages, each with 20 to 30 longhouses. The French mounted two more expeditions against the Iroquois in the late 1600s: against the Mohawks in 1693 and against the Onondagas and Oneidas in 1696.

Eighteenth Century
In 1701, the Iroquois Confederacy established peace with the British and the French that lasted until mid-century. The Confederacy continued to play the British off against the French and the French against the British. The Senecas did not rebuild Ganondagan after its destruction by de Nonville. People of the eastern village of Senecas moved farther eastward, establishing a village at the foot of Canandaigua Lake and another, the principal village, at the foot of Seneca Lake. Smaller villages were built along both sides of Seneca Lake and along the Chemung River.

People of the western Seneca village moved to fertile land along the Genesee River near Cuylerville. Also, they migrated northward along the Genesee River and southwesterly along the Allegheny River to Fort Pitt and into Ohio. Because it was a time of peace, their new villages were not palisaded. From 1726 to 1750, the British concentrated their trading efforts at Oswego, and the French built a fort at Niagara to control traffic between Lakes Erie and Ontario.

The western Senecas allied with the French during the French and Indian War (1754-1763) and joined Pontiac in his uprising against the British in 1763. They fought with the French at Fort Presque Isle near Erie, Pennsylvania, and at Fort Niagara. The eastern Senecas allied with the British during the French and Indian War and allowed Sir William Johnson to build a fort at Kanadesaga (Geneva).

In 1777, the Senecas sided with the British in attacking Fort Stanwix (Rome) and, the following year, joined them in the Wyoming and Cherry Valley massacres. The British attempted to destroy crops in the region, one of the breadbaskets of Washington's Colonial Army during the Revolutionary War. In addition to the destruction of villages of the Senecas and other Iroquois Nations in the Finger Lakes Region by Major General John Sullivan, Colonel Daniel Brodhead led an expedition eastward and northward along the Allegheny River, destroying all Seneca settlements that he found.

Following Sullivan's destruction of their villages and crops, many Senecas fled to Niagara, where they suffered during the extremely severe winter of 1779-80. The Iroquois participated in raids against the Colonials until the end of the Revolutionary War. In the Treaty of Paris of 1783 that ended the war, no provisions were made for the Iroquois Confederacy. In 1784, many Iroquois, including Senecas, moved to the Six Nations Reservation along the Grand River in Ontario, Canada.

Also that year, the Iroquois Confederacy met with Federal Government officials at Fort Stanwix and were forced to cede much of their land in western New York and Pennsylvania. The Six Nations contested this treaty. In 1794, the Iroquois met with U.S. Government representative Timothy Pickering in Canandaigua, where another treaty was signed that defined the boundaries of Seneca lands. It also documented land reserved for the Cayugas, Oneidas, and Onondagas in their treaties with the State of New York.

In 1786 in Hartford, Connecticut, the Commonwealth of Massachusetts was granted the pre-emptive right to buy land that the Iroquois had been granted in treaties; however, the land was to become part of the sovereignty of New York State. In 1788, Massachusetts sold these pre-emptive rights to land speculators Oliver Phelps and Nathaniel Gorham for $1 million in Massachusetts scrip. Also that year, the Senecas sold their land east of the Genesee River, including a small parcel west of the river, to Phelps and Gorham for $5,000 and $500 per year.

Because Massachusetts scrip appreciated in value, Phelps and Gorham were unable to pay the Commonwealth of Massachusetts for the pre-emptive rights, and the rights reverted to Massachusetts. In 1791, the Commonwealth resold the pre-emptive rights for $225,000 to Philadelphia banker Robert Morris, who sold them during the next two years to the Holland Land Company that had been established by trustees of Dutch banks. However, Morris had to clear Seneca land claims before the Holland Land Company would make any payments.

In 1796, the Commonwealth of Pennsylvania gave Seneca Chief Cornplanter a small tract of land on both sides of the Allegheny River south of the Allegany Reservation for services rendered. Cornplanter had played a significant role in convincing the Senecas not to join an association of western Indians in 1790-91. The deed to the land was passed on to Cornplanter's heirs.

On September 15, 1797, Senecas signed the Treaty of Big Tree, which deeded most of their lands to Morris for $100,000. They reserved 310 square miles on which their villages were located and 10 additional tracts: four reservations in western New York and six small ones totaling 26 square miles along the Genesee River. The Buffalo Creek Reservation, which housed Senecas, Cayugas, and Onondagas, had an area of 130 square miles, and the Tonawanda Creek Reservation had 71 square miles. The other two reservations of 42 square miles each were along the Allegheny River and Cattaraugus Creek.

Nineteenth Century

In 1798, the Society of Friends (Quakers) began to teach the "arts of civilization" to the Seneca Nation. Earlier missionary attempts with the Senecas by Jesuits and by Protestants had failed. Protestant missionary Samuel Kirkland gave up trying to convert the Senecas and founded a mission among the Oneidas. The Quaker mission at the Allegany Reservation remained in operation for over 100 years. In the early 1800s, other Protestant missionary attempts among the Senecas by the Western Missionary Society of Pittsburgh and by the New York Missionary Society at Buffalo Creek were short-lived.

In 1821, the United Foreign Missionary Society, which had absorbed the New York Missionary Society, sent a representative to Buffalo Creek. The mission was active until 1846 when the Buffalo Creek Reservation was sold, and the mission was moved to Cattaraugus. In 1822, the United Foreign Missionary Society established a school on the Cattaraugus Reservation. Churches were established at Cattaraugus in 1827 and at Allegany in 1830. In 1829, a Baptist church was established on the Tonawanda Reservation. In 1870, these missions were transferred to the Presbyterian Board of Missions.

In 1803, the Senecas sold Little Beard's Town on the Genesee River. In 1810, the Holland Land Company sold the rights to buy the rest of the Seneca reservations to David A. Ogden of the Ogden Land Company. In 1826, much of the Buffalo Creek, Cattaraugus, and Tonawanda Reservations were sold along with the remaining Seneca property along the Genesee River. In 1838, the Seneca Nation sold what was left of the Allegany, Buffalo Creek, Cattaraugus, and Tonawanda Reservations to the Ogden Land Company in a transaction signed by fewer than half of the chiefs. Sixteen of the chiefs who signed the bill of sale had been bribed. A treaty signed in 1842 negated the 1838 bill of sale.

In 1848, Senecas on the Allegany and Cattaraugus Reservations petitioned the U.S. Government to distribute their annuities directly to families instead of through the chiefs. This petition, referred to as a revolution, severed ties among the Allegany, Cattaraugus, and Tonawanda Reservations. During the 1840s and 1850s, the Tonawanda Senecas fought to keep their reservation. Finally, in 1857, 7,549 acres of the reservation were returned to the Tonawanda Senecas.

LEGENDS

The Serpent of Bare Hill

The Senecas lived in peace until a young Seneca boy found a small two-headed snake in the woods on Bare Hill. Bare Hill, called "Genundowa" by Native Americans, is located on the east side of Canandaigua Lake across the lake from a point five miles north of Woodville. Its summit, 865 feet above Canandaigua Lake, was the site of Seneca council fires.

The young Seneca boy made a pet of the snake, named it "Osaista Wanna," and initially fed it flies and frogs. As it grew, he gave it raccoons, squirrels, and woodchucks, and soon was feeding it large cuts of venison. Unfortunately, the serpent's appetite was insatiable. The boy could not find enough food to satisfy it, and the tribe began to fear the snake. They suspected that it was a monster.

Eventually, the immense snake surrounded the hill. When members of the tribe attempted to leave to obtain food, they were devoured by the huge two-headed serpent. Finally, a young boy and his sister were the only remaining members of the tribe. The boy had a dream one night that if he fletched his arrows with his sister's hair instead of feathers, the arrows would possess a lethal power to subdue the serpent.

The next day he fired his charmed arrows into the reptile's heart. The serpent, fatally wounded, writhed in agony as it rolled down Bare Hill, tearing out all of the bushes and trees and finally sliding into the lake. The snake disgorged the skulls of the Senecas that he had devoured, which was how the Senecas explained the large number of round, head-shaped stones found at the base of Bare Hill.

The Legend of Onnolee

The legend of Onnolee predates the time when Senecas dominated the country south of present-day Rochester. Between 1350 and 1375, a small tribe of friendly Indians, the Munsees, lived in the area between Hemlock and Canadice Lakes. They were surrounded by another tribe, the Mengwees. The Mengwees were a warlike tribe; nevertheless, the two tribes lived in peace. However, one night the Mengwees attacked the Munsees without warning and annihilated them. Onnolee, whom some said was a maiden and others said was the wife of the bravest chief, was the only survivor. She was bound to the red belt of Mickinac, a Mengwee chief, and carried off.

At noon the following day, they rested at a spreading oak to eat their mid-day meal of parched corn and smoke-dried venison. While Mickinac was eating, Onnolee grabbed his knife from his belt and swiftly buried it in his side. The young woman knew that her life had been forfeited; she ran as fast as she could while arrows whizzed by her from all directions. She reached a craggy bluff overlooking the nearby lake and, according to poet W. H. C. Hosmer:

> Regardless of the whizzing storm
> Of missiles raining round her
> Imploring eye she then upcast,
> And a low, mournful death hymn sang;
> On hill and forest she looked her last,
> One glance upon the water cast,
> And from that high rock sprang.

31

For over 300 years after her leap into the lake to her death, the form of the beautiful Onnolee could be seen rising out of the lake in the still of a summer night, either disappearing into the sky or returning to her watery home.

The "Drums" of Seneca Lake

The occasional booming sounds along Seneca Lake are difficult to explain. Many residents along the lake have never heard the "drums" of Seneca Lake. Other lakers have heard the booming noises many times. The sounds are heard most frequently around dusk in the late summer and early fall. They have been heard most distinctly near Dresden, on the west side of the lake, and near Lodi Point, on the east side.

Speculation is that the "popping" noises are caused by natural gas being released from fissures in the rocks at the bottom of the lake. This theory is supported by the fact that the boom of the drums was fainter in the 1920s when natural gas fields were developed around Tyrone, between Keuka and Seneca Lakes. When pumping from the Tyrone gas fields was discontinued, the previous volume returned to the booming sounds along Seneca Lake.

Senecas who used to live around the lake interpreted the noise as the sound of drums. They attempted to explain the sound as the drums of their forefathers, as the outward expression of evil spirits, or as signals from the God of Thunder. Many area residents believe that the "drums" are loudest just prior to a natural disaster, such as the severe flooding of Watkins Glen in 1935.

The Wandering Chief

One summer day, Agayenthah, a tall, young Seneca chief, known as the "Wandering Chief," was tracking a bear along a cliff at the edge of Seneca Lake. A sudden summer storm caused him to seek shelter under a large tree at the edge of the cliff. Lightning struck the tree, and both the chief and the tree received a fatal blow from the God of Thunder. They fell into the lake and floated, together, toward the middle of the lake.

The following day, another storm arose, and the Seneca Lake drums were heard. The trunk of a large tree was seen floating on the surface of the lake, riding high in the water and reminding viewers of a funeral barge. It was seen many times, always in the calm that precedes a storm. It was seen so often that when the Seneca drums are heard, people say that the Wandering Chief is on the trail again.

The Seneca's Curse

A Seneca legend about Keuka Lake tells of the occasional stormy moods of the usually calm and pleasant lake. Years ago, during the moon of the strawberry harvest, a young Seneca was crossing the lake with his wife and child when a sudden storm caused their canoe to capsize. It was dark, and his wife and daughter slipped under the surface of the water before he could save them. The storm passed, the lake became calm, and the empty canoe drifted toward him, driven by a slight breeze. The broken-hearted young man shook his fist in anger at the lake and cursed it:

> Today you seemed to smile. Your silky eyes laughed when my child and my wife dipped their fingers in your waters. You seemed to join us in thanking the Good Spirit for the coming of summer and the gift of strawberries, first fruit of the earth. But you lied. You are a snake. You have taken my family. Therefore, I curse you always to be hungry when the fifth moon is in the sky. You will catch and drown helpless women and children. For you will be hungry for them. I curse you to be unable to eat them. They will come to the top of the water and the wind will blow them to shore. I curse you always to be hungry when the fifth moon glows in the sky, and strawberries are ripe in the dark woods.

It is said that when summer storms cause a rare tragedy on Keuka Lake, the bodies always drift to the shore because of the Seneca's curse.

The Spirit Boatman

Iroquois paintings decorate the rock cliff along the eastern shore of Seneca Lake, near Hector. As told in Iroquois legend, the paintings were the work of a small Seneca war party that escaped a much larger contingent of soldiers of General Sullivan's Army during the Revolutionary War. According to the story, the outnumbered braves

33

were pursued and driven to the top of the cliffs along the lakeshore where the soldiers thought that they had the Senecas trapped.

The Senecas descended to the lake using a narrow path cut into the rock of the cliff. They risked their lives but safely reached the canoes that they had left at the base of the cliff. General Sullivan's men decided not to endanger their lives by following them down the hazardous path. The Senecas were so thankful for escaping from the soldiers that they went back later and created the cliffside paintings to commemorate the incident.

The legend adds that the Spirit Boatman represents the specter of one of the braves who escaped from General Sullivan's men. He appears as a Seneca warrior paddling his canoe near the rocks along the lakeshore in the moonlight.

The Attempt to Save the Algonquin

During skirmishes between the Senecas and the Algonquins from the north, an Algonquin chief was captured and taken to the Seneca village of Genundowa. The strong, young chief was condemned to death by impalement. While he was awaiting his fate in the cabin of death, his food was brought to him by Wun-nut-hay, the daughter of a Seneca chief. She was impressed by his manly bearing and became determined to help him to escape his sentence. She came to his cabin by the first light of dawn and easily slipped past the lone guard, who had fallen asleep. She cut the rawhide thongs that bound him and told him to come with her.

They followed the path down to the lake but, before they reached it, heard the alarm given by the awakened guard. They leaped into the canoe stored there by the young Seneca maiden for their escape and paddled furiously across the lake. However, 12 war canoes powered by muscular braves set out in pursuit. The young brave and the maiden landed on the opposite shore, ran uphill from the lake, and headed west. The young Algonquin, who was weakened by wounds that had not healed, followed his guide as fast as he could. Their pursuers, led by the old sachem, the maiden's father, rapidly gained on them.

The young woman realized that they were going to be overtaken, so she left the trail and led her companion to the crest of a cliff that was 150 feet above a rock-filled ravine. They could see the eagle-feather-plumed sachem and his party below them leaping from rock to rock. She called out to her father, who hesitated and then placed an arrow in his bow. The beautiful maiden placed herself between the young Algonquin and her father. She appealed to the sachem to spare the life of the young chief; she told her father that they would jump into the ravine together rather than be captured.

The old sachem disregarded her pleas; he ordered his men to climb to the top of the cliff and seize them. Just as the Senecas reached the precipice, the young couple embraced each other, leaped from the cliff, and perished on the rocks. They were buried at the base of the glen in the shade of large boulders. The two sunken graves are in a pleasant glade near a murmuring brook.

The Legend of Red Wing

Red Wing, daughter of a Seneca chief, frequently accompanied her parents on hunting and fishing trips to a place with rolling hills along the "Trail of the Senecas." Her favorite spot along the trail was a cool, moist glen with moss-covered rocks, wild grapevines, and towering trees that provided a heavy, green canopy.

Red Wing was courted, in Iroquois fashion, by two young Seneca men, Lone Pine and Sun Fish. Lone Pine was the suitor chosen by Red Wing, and soon after their marriage they walked along a trail through Red Wing's favorite glen with a party of Senecas from their tribe. They arrived at a high, dangerous part of the trail, and the jealous Sun Fish pushed the unsuspecting Lone Pine over the precipice. Just before Lone Pine went over the edge, he grabbed Sun Fish by the ankle and pulled him to death with him.

Before the party realized what was happening, Red Wing uttered a piercing cry, plunged over the cliff, and was united with her husband in death. The glen where Lone Pine, Red Wing, and Sun Fish joined the Great Spirit is in Stony Brook State Park near Dansville.

The Legend of the River

Tonadahwa, a beautiful Seneca maiden, was paddling her canoe down the river far from her village one afternoon when she thought that she heard her intended husband call to her. He had once risked his life to save her from danger, and she had eyes only for him. She steered for the bank to join him when another young man, one of her spurned suitors, jumped into her canoe with a look of triumph on his face. He grabbed her paddle and tried to take control of the canoe when suddenly he was struck in the chest by an arrow. He jumped out of the canoe with the paddle in his hands and pushed the canoe out into the rapids.

Tonadahwa's canoe moved through the rapids at great speed. She chanted her death-song and waved goodbye to her lover on the shore. Her husband-to-be raced along the bank to the waterfall downstream. He jumped into the waterfall from a high bank when he could no longer see the canoe in the rapids. The Spirit of the River caught the young man, saved him from death, and put him on a ledge at the bottom of the falls where Tonadahwa was placed in his arms.

He walked through the raging waterfall carrying his prospective bride to safety. When the unconscious maiden awakened, both she and her intended thanked the Great Spirit for their safety. The Senecas claimed that if you walked by the waterfall, you could hear, against a background of rushing water and murmuring pines, the doleful cry of the young man as he jumped into the waterfall.

The Tree of Silver Arrows

A Seneca father and his two sons left their longhouse to travel to the edge of the earth and then across Crystal Lake to the Land of the Great Spirit. On the shore of the large lake, they encountered three eagles who offered to convey them across the waters. The three Senecas rode the backs of the eagles to the Land of the Great Spirit. When they landed on the far shore of Crystal Lake, they encountered young men, maidens, and chiefs who had been chained there by the Great Spirit. A breathtakingly beautiful maiden was chained with the others. The younger son fell in love with her the moment that he saw her, and he could tell from her eyes that his love was reciprocated.

The father and his sons stayed in the Land of the Great Spirit for three days. The younger son courted the beautiful maiden and pleaded with her to come to his village and share his lodge. She told him, through her tears, that she could not go with him because she was of the Land of the Great Spirit and could not return to Earth Land. The way that they could be together, she said, was for him to return to earth and wait for the call of death from the Great Spirit.

Only then could they be together.

When the father and his sons prepared to leave for home, the younger son could not be found. They searched for him in shaded groves, in hidden valleys, and in the silvery forest. They found him lying at the base of the Tree of Silver Arrows, which had silver shafts instead of branches and silver arrow tips in place of leaves. He had pulled one of the silver arrows from the tree and thrust it into his heart. The lovesick young man had found a way to join his loved one in the Land of the Great Spirit.

The Legend of Heno

Heno, the God of Thunder, was one of the great gods of the Iroquois. He was considered second in importance only to the Great Spirit; in some histories of the Iroquois, the God of Thunder and the Great Spirit were considered one being. The God of Thunder, or "He-great-voice," was the maker of rain and storms. When he wrinkled his forehead, thunder could be heard. When he blinked his eyes, lightning would shoot toward the earth.

The God of Thunder was the enemy of all evil spirits. He intimidated the malevolent beings of the underworld and forced them to return to their caves. His goals were to kill all malicious creatures that used evil magic and then to slay the underwater serpent.

One legend about Heno involved his pursuit of the evil serpent that was poisoning the springs of Senecas in western New York State. The monster serpent was as long as 20 arrow flights. The malicious serpent lived underground along a river and came out at night to spread his poison into the tribe's drinking water. Heno found the serpent causing destruction one night and killed him with bolts of lightning that were like arrows of fire. The huge serpent squirmed and twisted in pain.

Men of the tribe dragged the writhing, nearly spent body of the evil serpent to the river and threw him in. In his death throes, the serpent flailed over the precipice of a huge waterfall, enlarging it and changing its shape forever.

Tonawanda Indian Community House, Tonawanda Reservation

Cayuga Museum, Iroquois Center, Auburn

CHAPTER 2

THE CAYUGA NATION

"As a nation, the Cayuga are regarded as offshoots of either the Mohawk or the Seneca. Their name in the League was 'So-ne-na-we-too-na, or Great Pipe,' as this object was their emblem. The name Iroquois is also said to have come from Ierowka or 'those who smoke.' Therefore, the Cayuga may be the oldest in derivation from the parent stock of 1535 on the St. Lawrence River, or the western one from which they also descended. Kept alive in prehistoric—as in historic—time, by intermarriage after decimating conflicts, they survived in tradition as descendants from either the Mohawk or Seneca, with whom they repeatedly mixed."

Grace Ellis Taft, *Cayuga Notes*

HISTORY

The Cayuga Nation, one of the younger brothers of the Iroquois Confederacy along with the Oneidas and Tuscaroras, lived in the region between the Senecas, Keepers of the Western Door, and the Onondagas, Keepers of the Council Fire. They occupied the land between Cayuga and Owasco Lakes, which is now Cayuga County. The region in which they hunted included the land around Cayuga and Owasco Lakes northward to Lake Ontario and southward toward the Susquehanna River. Because game and fish were plentiful, they relied more on hunting and fishing than on raising crops.

Seventeenth Century

The Cayugas had three main villages: Thiohero and Onontaré on the Seneca River and Oiogouen, near Great Gully Brook, south of present-day Union Springs. Thiohero, where Jesuits established the Mission of Ste. Estienne, was located 12 miles from Oiogouen, near the outlet of Cayuga Lake. Jesuits built another mission, the Mission of Ste. René, at Onontaré, 18 miles from Oiogouen. In 1668, a third mission, the Mission of Ste. Joseph, was established. By 1677, the three villages had been moved to within a mile of one another, several miles from Cayuga Lake.

During the first half of the 17th century, the Iroquois nations, including the Cayugas, depended on the fur trade to obtain European goods. When fewer beaver were available in their hunting territories, they fought with neighboring nations to obtain pelts. In 1649, the Senecas and the Mohawks defeated the Hurons, and the Iroquois expanded their trapping territory. Peace with the French was established in 1653. Jesuits established the Mission of Ste. Marie among the Onondagas three years later. Father René Ménard attempted to found a mission among the Cayugas but was unsuccessful. He left Iroquois territory in 1658.

In the 1660s, Senecas, Cayugas, and Onondagas fought the Susquehannocks to the south. Some Cayugas moved to the Bay of Quinté in Canada to escape war with the Susquehannocks. A Cayuga chief represented his nation and the Onondagas in another peace negotiation with the French in Montreal. The Iroquois did not want to have enemies both to the south and to the north at the same time.

Father Simon Le Moyne visited the Cayugas while staying with the Onondagas in 1662. Two years later, a Cayuga delegation on a visit to Quebec requested missionaries. The Jesuits' plan to travel to Cayuga country was thwarted in 1666 by the French general de Tracy's attack on the Mohawks. However, the Jesuits made the trip two years later to establish the Mission of Ste. Joseph at the Cayuga village of Oiogouen. Some captured Hurons and Susquehannocks lived with the Cayugas at the time. Opposition to the Jesuits caused the priests to leave Iroquois country again in 1682.

The peace with the French was another temporary peace. In 1687, de Nonville attacked the Senecas and burned their villages. In 1693, the French attacked the Mohawks and destroyed their settlements, followed, three years later, by Louis de Frontenac's destruction of Onondaga and Oneida villages. The Cayugas were the only Iroquois nation that escaped attack by the French.

Eighteenth Century

The century began with another peace with the French in 1701. The Cayugas were sufficiently confident of their safety that they did not build palisades around their villages. Cayuga villages were moved again. In addition to a village on the Seneca River and on the east side of Cayuga Lake, they built a village on the west side of Cayuga Lake and one to the south toward the Susquehanna River. In 1750, their principal village on the east side of Cayuga Lake was visited by Moravians.

The Cayugas attempted, unsuccessfully, to remain neutral during the Revolutionary War. Led by their distinguished chief, Fish Carrier, they fought as allies of the British. While the main body of Major General John Sullivan's army destroyed Seneca longhouses, crops, and stored grain, two detachments destroyed Cayuga property: Colonel Henry Dearborn burned Cayuga villages on the west side of Cayuga Lake, and Colonel William Butler destroyed those on the east side.

After the Revolutionary War, some Cayugas moved to the Six Nations Reservation along the Grand River in Canada, while others lived with the Senecas on the Buffalo Creek Reservation. In 1790, 130 Cayugas lived on both sides of Cayuga Lake, toward the northern end of the lake. When these lands were sold, they moved with

Chief Fish Carrier to the Grand River Reservation in Ontario, Canada.

In the Treaty of Albany in 1789, the Cayugas sold all of their land in New York State to the State except for a 100-square-mile tract at the northern end of Cayuga Lake, extending from Aurora to Montezuma. This land was sold to the State, except for a two-mile-square tract south of Union Springs and a one-square-mile tract on the east side of Cayuga Lake, in the Treaty of Cayuga Ferry in 1795. Also, Chief Fish Carrier was granted a one-square-mile tract at Canoga on the west side of Cayuga Lake in this treaty.

Nineteenth Century

In 1807, the two small tracts on the east side of Cayuga Lake were sold to New York State, and, in 1841, Chief Fish Carrier's property on the west side of the lake was sold to the State. After selling their land in the late 1700s, many Cayugas, along with other Iroquois, moved to the Lower Sandusky River area in Ohio. They fought as allies of the Americans in the War of 1812.

In 1817, in a treaty signed at the foot of the rapids of the Miami River, those Iroquois were given 30,000 acres along the Sandusky River. The site, known as the Seneca Sandusky Reservation, was enlarged to 40,000 acres the following year. In 1829, 157 Cayugas lived on the reservation. In 1831, the Sandusky Senecas sold their reservation and moved to northeastern Oklahoma.

In 1838, the Iroquois sold all their land in New York State, over the objections of many Cayugas. Because of this opposition, another treaty was signed in 1842 in which the Cattaraugus and Allegany Reservations were retained. Many Iroquois, including Cayugas, living at Buffalo Creek moved to the Cattaraugus Reservation when the Buffalo Creek Reservation was sold. By the end of the 19th century, most of the Cayugas who lived in New York State lived on three Seneca reservations, principally the Cattaraugus Reservation, and on the Onondaga Reservation.

LEGENDS

The Legend of Ensenore

The legend of Ensenore begins with the destruction of an Indian village at what is now Schenectady by a marauding band of Cayuga Indians. Ensenore, a young brave from the village destroyed by the Cayugas, fought well, but his tribe was outnumbered by the invaders. After the battle, Ensenore looked for his betrothed, Kathreen, and was told that she had been carried off by the Cayugas, who returned westward toward Owasco Lake.

He followed them, after disguising himself so that the Cayugas would not associate him with his village at Schenectady. He wore a fur cap with a red plume, dressed gaudily, painted his face, and hung pendants from his ears. The Cayugas avoided the Great Trail of the Iroquois on their return home, because they expected to be pursued by a band seeking revenge. When Kathreen collapsed with fatigue, the Cayugas carried her on a litter made of boughs and leaves.

After three days, the Cayuga warriors reached their home on the shore of Owasco Lake, described by Peter Meyers in his poem, "Ensenore," from *The Lakes & Legends of Central New York* by J. O. Noyes:

> Their favorite Western hunting ground,
> Upon the shore of that fair lake,
> Whose waters are the clearest, brightest;
> Whose silver surges ever break
> Upon her pebbled margin, lightest:
> ....
> Owasco's waters sweetly slept,
> Owasco's banks were bright and green.
> The willow on her margin wept,
> The wild fowl on her wave were seen.
> And nature's golden charms were shed,
> As richly round her quiet bed,
> From flowered mead to mountain brow,
> A century since, as they are now;
> The same pure, purple light was flung
> At morn, across the water's breast;

43

> The same rich crimson curtains hung
> At eve around the glowing west,
> But seldom then the white man's eye
> Imbibed the beauties of that view;
> Unnoticed, spread the cloudless sky
> Its canopy of spotless blue
> Unnoticed, back to Heaven, the wave
> That azure sky's pure semblance gave.

Ensenore knew the location of the Cayuga village on Owasco Lake, so he passed the village and doubled back to approach it from the west by canoe. Ensenore entered the largest longhouse, was extended the courtesies of a guest, and smoked the ceremonial pipe as it was passed around. Kathreen did not recognize him. Ensenore told stories about his tribe, which he said was from far to the west. The Cayugas told Ensenore of their recent expedition and of the rescue of a beautiful Indian maiden from an upraised knife by their chief, Eagle Eye. Eagle Eye had told them to treat her as his future wife.

A few days later, Kathreen was permitted to retire to a secluded place on the lakeshore to weep alone. The gaudily-dressed brave approached to speak with her. She was startled and fled back to the camp before Ensenore could identify himself.

Eagle Eye returned to camp that evening and joined in the storytelling; he told stories about the recent raid and smoked the ceremonial pipe. During the revelry, Ensenore passed a small packet identifying himself to Kathreen, who sighed and uttered his name. On his way out of the longhouse, Ensenore whispered to her to be ready to leave that night. Kathreen made it past the sentry, but Ensenore's escape was discovered; the camp was alerted.

When the couple reached the cove where Ensenore had left his canoe, they found that a slight breeze had caused it to drift out from the shore. They waded to the canoe but were seen in the moonlight. Ensenore headed southward, paddling rapidly; the Cayugas were close behind them. When the moon went behind the clouds, Ensenore changed direction and steered toward the northern end of the lake. They escaped the pursuing Cayugas, had an uneventful three-day trip back to Schenectady, and were married. Presumably, they lived happily ever after.

The Door at Taughannock Falls

When observing the 215-foot-high falls from the overlook in Taughannock Falls State Park, visitors can envision the outline of a door high on the wall of the ravine to the right of the waterfall. The Iroquois considered it a mystery of nature that they could not explain, so they created a legend about it.

Chief Ganungueguch and his tribe lived along what would later be called Taughannock Creek in the area of the waterfall many years before White men entered the region. The Iroquois were continually at war with the Delawares from Pennsylvania. Chief Taughannock and his Delawares raided the Cayugas and Senecas in the region and were defeated.

Chief Taughannock and most of his men were killed, but some Delawares survived and were adopted by their captors. One of the adopted Delawares fell in love with White Lily, a Cayuga maiden. The Cayuga men were jealous and watched the pair closely to prevent them from running away together.

One dark night, the two lovers ran toward the Delaware's canoe on the shore of Cayuga Lake. They planned to escape southward to Delaware country. An early alarm frustrated their attempt to escape. They did not know whether a jealous suitor or the barking of one of the tribe's dogs alerted the village. Soon, many Cayugas from the village were chasing them through the pine forest.

From the shouts of those in pursuit, the couple knew that they would be overtaken before reaching the ford across the creek above the falls. They ran from the protection of the pine forest and could be seen in the moonlight. They stood on the edge of the falls, embraced, and leapt to what they thought was certain death on the jagged rocks below. They preferred death to capture and the torture that would be inflicted on the young Delaware according to the code of the Iroquois. The villagers gathered near the pinnacle from which they had jumped; the women of the tribe wailed at the death of the maiden. When the lamentations subsided, the people returned to the village. They planned to return to the base of the falls to bury the young couple in the morning.

When the villagers returned to the site of the pair's death after dawn, however, they found no mangled bodies nor any trace of the Delaware and the maiden. The tribe's storytellers said that the Great Spirit was aware of the young couple's love and of their attempt to elope and sympathized with them. He opened the door high on the side of the ravine and, when they jumped, ushered them through the secret passageway and closed the door tightly. The passageway led to a domain where White Lily and her Delaware lover could live in peace and happiness forever.

The Legend of Pine Cone

Before the formation of the Iroquois Confederacy, the Five Nations fought among themselves. At a time when the Cayuga and Seneca Nations were at war, a young Cayuga man, Pine Cone, fell in love with the daughter of a Seneca chief. He wanted to marry her, but her tribe would not allow it. Pine Cone had to rely on a ruse to carry off his intended to marry her. He sent his fellow Cayugas in canoes to Canoga, on the west side of Cayuga Lake, to appear to be staging an attack.

The Senecas quickly discovered his deception and pursued Pine Cone and the Seneca maiden in their canoe. As Pine Cone paddled across Cayuga Lake, he began to tire because he was rowing for two. He would have been overtaken if the Great Spirit had not created an island, Frontenac Island, between him and the pursuing Senecas. The obstacle of the island gave Pine Cone time to escape to the eastern shore of the lake with the Seneca maiden.

Frontenac Island, one of two islands in the Finger Lakes (Squaw Island in Canandaigua Lake is the other), lies one-half mile off Union Springs on the eastern shore of Cayuga Lake. The island, consisting of Cobbleskill limestone, is less than an acre in size and is elevated eight feet above lake level.

The Legend of Lake Eldridge

The Iroquois village of Shinedowa stood on the site of present-day Elmira. The village was surrounded by cornfields, plum trees, and apple orchards. Unusually shaped mounds that had been formed by flood waters were located south of the village along the Chemung River. Beyond these mounds were evergreen trees that hid the village's burial grounds. The mounds and the evergreens were the gates to the happy hunting ground. The women of the tribe went there to weep for their dead relatives and friends.

Mt. Zoar dominated the surrounding hills. The council house was located in the center of the plain. The women sat on the ground around the council house braiding rushes into multi-colored mats, making moccasins, and weaving baskets. As they worked, they traded news. One day, the chief's wife observed that her son, Owenah, had the evil eye. The chief had gone to Seneca Castle a moon ago. Upon his return, she knew that he planned to convene the council to discuss the spell that had been cast over their son.

Another woman replied that even the children could tell that there was something wrong with the chief's son. A third woman noted that the girls of the village avoided Owenah because his strange behavior scared them. This woman thought that her friend's son was definitely under an evil spell. The chief's wife reminded her friends that Owenah was always reserved, shy, and a little strange, but that they had hoped that he would settle down and become a great chief like his father. However, for the last six months, he had done nothing to prepare himself to become a warrior or to hunt for the tribe.

According to *O-WE-NAH, A Legend of Lake Eldridge*, an adaptation by William Heidt, Jr., an Iroquois woman said:

> Once no young brave could cope with Owenah in the hunt, and he was known in the lodges from Seneca to Tioga as among the bravest. But he has changed. He sits as idle as the painted leaves. He listens no more to the stories of war. His bows and arrows are neglected. He sharpens not his knife, and he goes no longer to the lodge of the arrow maker for arrows. The younger braves look upon him with distrust, and the girls laugh at him or look at him askance, but he does not mind it. The old warriors have noticed his strange ways and say he will never be a warrior unless he rouses from his slumber.

Most of the tribe agreed with the observation that the evil eye was upon him.

Every day, Owenah went into the swamps surrounding the bottomless lake that the tribe called "Ouwela." He took no weapons with him, and he returned empty handed with a distant look in his eye. The pride of the tribe had changed, and he was now a disappointment to his community. The village had hoped that Owenah

47

would take over as chief when his father became too infirm to lead. However, during the last few months, Owenah had become reserved and quiet, had avoided his friends, and had given up the hunt.

When his companions asked him to join the chase for wild game, he gave them vague excuses. He returned at the end of the day with no fish, game, or edible roots. When asked what he had done all day, he avoided the question. The rest of the tribe stayed away from the swamp because they considered it evil. In the past, many men had been lured to the swamp by voices that called them and fires that attracted them. They were never heard from again. The green Piasau, or "bird of doom," was known to go there; its eerie cry on dark nights had spread terror through the village.

Several years earlier, a band of hunters from the village had forced their way through the thicket to the shores of the lake, where one of the bravest had been seized by a terrifying monster that came up from the depths. The young man was pulled down into the lake and was never seen again. The rest of the party escaped, but they heard the cry of the Piasau as they returned to the village. They were terrified of this cry because they knew that the bird of doom could carry away a man with the ease of an eagle carrying a fish.

Men of the tribe had sunken hundreds of feet of line into the lake and had found no bottom. Geese did not rest on the dark surface of the lake either on their migration southward or on their return northward in the spring. No one but Owenah visited the bottomless body of water. The rest of the tribe wondered what interest he could possibly have in the lake. They did not know that when he had wandered into the swamp unintentionally about a year previously, he had stumbled upon a beautiful girl sitting on a fallen tree arranging a wreath of wild flowers. He had never seen such breathtaking beauty.

She was slender and dressed like the girls of his tribe, but the many ornaments on her dress indicated that she was a princess. She was fairer than the girls in his village, and her eyes had a tender gleam in them. Her black hair fell well below her shoulders. Owenah was captivated by her and could think of nothing to say. She asked him why his arrows had found no game. He responded that his companions were hunting on the other side of the hill, and he decided to see if he could find game on this side.

She pointed and said, "If Owenah will go to that tall pine in the distance, he will find game." He was so surprised to hear his name pronounced by a stranger and in such a sorrowful tone that he was filled with wonder. He turned in the direction that she had pointed; by the time that he turned back toward her, she had disappeared. He had heard no noise, and he could not tell in which direction she had gone. He was filled with awe. As he walked in the direction of the tall pine, he heard the call of the Kalewee, the "bird of evil omen." However, he could not think of anything but his beautiful companion. He saw nothing but her endearing image.

At the foot of the tall pine tree, Owenah saw a white deer, which he killed with a single arrow. He dragged the deer back to the village and placed it at his mother's feet. She told him that she feared that evil would happen to him, because he had killed an albino doe. She suggested that he tell no one about it.

Owenah could not get the beautiful girl by the lake out of his mind. He thought about her all the time; he was smitten. He returned many times to the fallen tree where he had seen her, but he always returned home disappointed. Winter came and went, and he did not find her by the lake. One spring day, he found her where he had seen her before. As before, she was arranging a garland of blossoms. She asked him why a hunter would come to the lake with its surrounding swamp; there were neither fish nor game there.

Owenah hesitated in answering, blushed, and answered that he had come looking for the chief's daughter who knew his name. He asked of what tribe her father was chief, and where his village was. She answered by pointing to Ouwela, the lake. Then she got up from the fallen tree and gestured for him to follow her toward the lake. He waded through the marshes and penetrated the thickets with difficulty, while the strikingly beautiful maiden made her way easily.

Her path led them into thicket and woods where the only light was an occasional glimmering of twilight through the leaves. They heard the cry of strange birds, and occasionally a snake would slither across the trail in front of them. Eventually, they came to the shore of the lake, where a canoe made of white bark was moored among the water lilies. She stepped into the canoe and pushed off from the shore. She pointed across the dark lake and said that her home was in that direction. She told him that her name was

49

Newamee, and that he should not try to follow her as her canoe moved into the mist.

Owenah visited their place in the woods daily, and he usually found her there. His friends taunted him continually for giving up the hunt and for wandering off by himself. However, the impact of these taunts was more than offset by seeing the object of his affections. He talked with her during the day and dreamed of her at night.

On many occasions, his friends followed him to see how he was spending his time. They were unable to find their old companion. Finally, two young men penetrated the thicket surrounding the mysterious lake and saw them in the white canoe. However, a black wolf came down the path toward them, and they ran back to the village as fast as they could. Both of them received serious injuries before the summer was over.

Owenah's bow and arrows hung unused on the wall of his parents' lodge. Summer passed into autumn, and one day Newamee was not at their meeting place. Little mist rose from the haunted lake that day, and he could see the white canoe on the other side of the lake. He called out her name, but the only answer he received was from a bird that seemed to mock him. He thought about some of the things that she had told him: that she lived adjacent to the big sea water, that large lodges floated on the water, and that bottomless Lake Ouwela had a huge cave that led to the big sea waters.

Newamee also had told him that she was the daughter of the Great Spirit, and that in time she would send for him. He did not know how to take these revelations; they filled him with apprehension. The next time that she met him at the lake, she had a very sad look on her face. She told him that he must not come to their meeting place again. She asked him if he had heard the cry of the Kalewee as he walked though the swamp. She told him that the cry of the bird of evil omen was intended as a warning to him.

Owenah placed his hand on Newamee's arm; he said that he would not have to come here anymore if she would agree to marry him and return with him to his lodge. She replied that she could not come to live with Owenah's tribe because there was a spell on her, and that she must return home. She reminded him that her home was to the north, and that she must return there though the large cave in Lake Ouwela that opened into Seneca Lake and eventually led to the big sea waters. She could do nothing to break the spell.

Owenah was stunned; he could not bear the possibility that they might be separated. His voice trembled, and he shuddered as he reached out for Newamee. However, she stepped into the canoe and paddled away from the shore. She told him that he could not come with him at that time, but that she would talk with the Great Spirit. If He agreed, she said that she would send the white canoe at the time of the next full moon.

As Newamee paddled away from the shore, the sky became dark and thunder could be heard in the distance. Owenah held out his arms and begged her to come back. She said no by shaking her head, and, as she reached the middle of the lake, lightning flashed, thunder boomed, and the winds rose. He saw her disappear; he could not find her when he waded into the water.

Owenah returned to his village. His family and neighbors could see that he was even more preoccupied than before. He went to the meeting place by the lake every day and called out to Newamee, but he received no reply and saw no white canoe. Finally, he failed to return home. After several days, a search party was sent out for him. They knew that they must risk going through the swamp to the lake to look for him. They found the lifeless Owenah lying in the bottom of a white bark canoe. The Great Spirit had called him to the place by the big sea waters.

The tribe buried him in a mound near Lake Ouwela. The villagers wailed the cry of the dead, "Oonah, oonah," as they buried him with his little-used weapons. His mother was nearly overcome with grief. The villagers visited his grave regularly, even though it was near the haunted lake.

Owenah still rests under the mound near the site of the village of Shinedowa on the plain with Mt. Zoar in the distance. However, his tribe has moved on, leaving little evidence of their stewardship of the land.

Onondaga Community Center, Onondaga Reservation

Onondaga Council House, Onondaga Reservation

CHAPTER 3

THE ONONDAGA NATION

"Atotarho, who by tradition was an Onondaga, is the great embodiment of the Iroquois courage, wisdom, and heroism, and he is invested with allegoric traits which exalt him to a kind of superhuman character. Unequalled in war and arts, his fame spread abroad and exalted the Onondaga Nation in the highest scale. He was placed at the head of the Confederacy, and his name was used after his death as an exemplar of glory and honor. While like that of Caesar, it became perpetuated as the official title of the presiding Sachem of the Confederacy."

Elias Johnson, *Legends, Traditions, and Laws of the Iroquois or Six Nations*

HISTORY

The Onondagas were the most geographically central nation of the Iroquois Confederacy. Senecas and Cayugas lived west of them and Tuscaroras, Oneidas, and Mohawks were located to the east. The Onondaga Nation, Keeper of the Fire of the Confederacy, was host for the councils and keeper of the wampum for the Six Nations. Because their brother nations protected them from attacks from the West and the East, their principal threats were the Hurons to the north and the Susquehannocks to the south. The Onondagas were strategically located between the French and their Indian allies (Petuns, Neutrals, and Eries) west of the Senecas and the Dutch, later English, in Albany east of the Mohawks.

Seventeenth Century

When the war between the Iroquois and the Eries began, the Onondagas decided to avoid war on two fronts. In 1653, they sent a delegation to Montreal to make peace with the French. In 1654, Jesuit Father Simon Le Moyne visited the Onondagas. Two years later, the Jesuits constructed the Mission of Ste. Marie at Gannentaha (Onondaga Lake), 15 miles from the main Onondaga village. The mission was abandoned in 1658, when the Jesuits learned that the Onondagas were going to destroy it.

Pro-French Onondagas invited Father Le Moyne to return in 1661. In 1666, after the French general de Tracy's destruction of Mohawk villages, the Iroquois again made peace with the French. Shortly afterward, the Mission of Ste. Jean Baptiste was built among the Onondagas.

War with the Susquehannocks was costly. Jesuits reported that the Onondagas lost a substantial number of warriors in the conflict, which ended in 1675. Onondaga villages were located near Butternut and Limestone Creeks between Onondaga Creek and Cazenovia Lake. They moved their villages every 10 to 20 years to be closer to their supplies of firewood. At any one time, they had only two villages, a large one where the councils of the Confederacy were held and a small one.

In 1677, the large village had 140 longhouses and the small one had 24. In 1681, the principal village was located on the east side of Butternut Creek, a mile south of today's Jamesville. Their hunt-

Sainte Marie Among the Iroquois, Syracuse

ing grounds encompassed all of what is now Onondaga County from Skaneateles Lake to Cazenovia Lake. They spanned the area from Lake Ontario in the north to Chenango Forks in the south.

Although the Onondagas were at peace with the French, they also conducted considerable trade with the British in Albany. During the 1680s, peace with the French deteriorated, and most of the Jesuit missionaries were withdrawn from Iroquois country. Peace with the French ended in 1687, when the Marquis de Nonville attacked the Senecas at Ganondagan. In 1696, Louis de Frontenac led an expedition against the Onondagas and the Oneidas and burned the principal Onondaga village.

Eighteenth Century

In 1701, peace was again negotiated with the French, and Jesuit missionaries returned to live among the Onondagas. They left again in 1708 when their chapel and mission house were burned. The French and the British destroyed each other's forts at the main Onondaga village. Finally, the British built a trading post at Oswego that was extremely successful, particularly in establishing fur trade with western New York.

By 1729, the Onondagas had moved their main settlement westward along Onondaga Creek. The size of Onondaga villages grew as they adopted Eries, Hurons, and Susquehannocks that they had defeated in battle.

David Zeisberger, a Moravian missionary, visited the Onondagas from 1750-1755, until driven out by the outbreak of the French and Indian War. In 1749, Abbé Francois Picquet, a Sulpician missionary, established a mission called "La Presentation," where the Owegatchie River flows into the St. Lawrence River, now Ogdensburg. In the 1750s, some Onondagas, Cayugas, and Oneidas moved there. Onondagas who moved north to La Presentation were called Oswegatchies, who, in 1754, fought in the French and Indian War alongside the French. During the Revolutionary War, they were allied with the British.

As the Revolutionary War approached, Onondagas who had stayed in central New York were pulled in three directions: some sided with the British, some with the Americans, and others wanted to remain neutral. The Onondagas fought as allies of the British. During the War, American Colonel Goose Van Schaik destroyed a ten-mile stretch of creekside Onondaga dwellings.

After the war, 225 Onondagas moved from central New York with the Mohawk chief, Joseph Brant, to the Six Nations Reservation in Canada, where an Iroquois Confederacy council fire was relit. Another council fire was rekindled by about 300 Onondagas, along with Senecas and Cayugas, at the Buffalo Creek Reservation. Only 140 Onondagas stayed at their original home near Onondaga Lake.

In 1788 by the Fort Schuyler Treaty, Onondagas sold all of their land in New York State except for a 100-square-mile tract in Onondaga County that included the land where Syracuse is today. In 1793, they sold about three-quarters of their tract; two years later by the Cayuga Ferry Treaty, they sold their rights to Onondaga Lake and the land around it.

Nineteenth Century

In 1806, the Oswegatchies were ordered by New York State to leave the Ogdensburg area. Many went to the St. Regis Reservation in Canada, and others moved back to Onondaga Lake. In the early 1800s, more Onondagas returned to join the 140 Onondagas who had stayed at their original home near Onondaga Lake. By the mid-1820s, 260 lived there; in the following decade, 310 lived at their homeland, while 94 resided at Buffalo Creek and 80 were at Allegany with the Senecas.

In 1817, Onondagas sold 4,320 acres on the east side of their reservation and 600 acres on the south side of the reservation to New York State for $33,360 and an annuity of $2,430. In 1838, Onondagas sold their remaining land in New York State but the sale was fraudulent, and they retained their reservation. However, the neighboring Oneidas sold their reservation, and those Oneidas who did not move to Canada lived on the Onondaga Reservation. As their land area decreased, Onondagas depended less on hunting for their livelihood and more on agriculture and on jobs with Whites, like the other Iroquois nations.

In 1847, when the Buffalo Creek Reservation was sold, the Onondaga council fire and wampum records were moved back to Onondaga. About 150 Onondagas remained on the Tuscarora and Seneca Reservations; most were at the Allegany Reservation.

Early in the 19th century, Onondagas heard Handsome Lake,

the Seneca medicine man, speak at the Buffalo Creek Reservation and were captivated by him. He influenced some Onondagas to abstain from drinking alcohol. In 1815, Handsome Lake died while visiting the Onondaga Reservation and is buried there. His grave, which was originally beneath the floor of the longhouse, is marked by a stone monument across the road from the Council House.

Eleazar Williams, a catechist who lived with the Mohawks, visited the Onondagas, as did Episcopal and Presbyterian clergymen. Quakers ran a school from 1828 to 1835, and, in 1848, Methodists built a church on the reservation. However, the Onondagas were not as attracted to Christianity as the Oneidas and Mohawks were. Many Onondagas were followers of the New Religion of Handsome Lake.

Onondagas continued to be Keepers of the Fire. Also, they were keepers of the wampum records of the Iroquois Confederacy until 1898, when the the remaining Onondaga wampum belts were transferred to the New York State Museum in Albany.

LEGENDS

The Legend of Hiawatha
Hiawatha, the great Onondaga chief and hunter, lived on the south shore of Cross Lake, west of Syracuse. In the "Song of Hiawatha," Henry Wadsworth Longfellow transported Hiawatha to the shores of Lake Gitche Gumee in Minnesota and made him a Ojibwa Indian via poetic license.

Hiawatha spoke to the chiefs of the Mohawk, Oneida, Onondaga, Cayuga, and Seneca Nations one day near present-day Liverpool on Onondaga Lake. The chiefs counted on Hiawatha to lead them to a more peaceful way of life. He held a single arrow in his outstretched hand and, facing the chiefs, broke the arrow over his knee. Next he took from his quiver five arrows that had been bound together with deerskin thongs. The five arrows represented the original Five Nations of the Iroquois Confederacy, and, when he tried to break them over his knee, he could not.

Hiawatha's demonstration of strength in unity was the underlying principle of the Iroquois Confederacy. The Iroquois maintained a strong confederacy for over 200 years, and hostile tribes, such as the Hurons and the Susquehannocks, provided a lesser threat than before the Confederacy was formed.

The Lost Onondaga Babe

Green Lake, called "Kai-yah-koo" by the Onondagas, is located in present-day Fayetteville, Onondaga County. Just under 200-foot deep, the lake is appropriately named. Its unique green color is due to its small amount of plant life and the presence of minimal suspended material in the water.

The legend begins with Laque, a young Onondaga woman, walking along the shore of the clear, deep lake, returning to her village from a visit to Oneida Castle. She was carrying her eight-month-old son and supplies for which she had bartered there. It was a hot day of the seventh moon as she walked the trail along the lake. As dusk approached, Laque stopped along the shore lined with marl- and moss-covered rocks. She looked forward to a rest as she removed the burden's trumpline across her forehead and rested her papoose against the root of a tree.

Laque lapsed wearily into a dream. She heard a noise in the bushes nearby and wondered if it were a wild animal or a devil of the evening. Then she saw a well-dressed woman emerge from the thicket. The stranger looked at Laque's baby and placed an infant that she carried on the ground next to him.

The beautiful woman told Laque of a difficult journey from her village to the south. She was a princess, the only daughter of a powerful sachem, and she had displeased her father and had been cast out from her tribe. Her father had killed her husband and intended to slay her child as well. She was exhausted from her journey. The stranger's voice was so soft and melodic that Laque was mesmerized by it. Laque was strongly moved by sympathy for the princess.

The richly dressed woman reminded Laque that the customs of their nation did not prevent the exchanging of children. She asked Laque to take her child, and said that she would take Laque's infant and raise him as her own. That way, her father would not attempt to kill the substituted child. At some point in the future, they could exchange the children back to their rightful parents. Laque saw that precious gems decorated the clothing of the son of the princess, and that he had eyes that sparkled brightly. Laque, who was tired and not thinking clearly, agreed to the exchange.

The princess quickly picked up Laque's infant and lifted him onto her shoulder. The infant smiled at his mother as the stranger carried him off into the forest. Laque placed the exchanged infant on her back and continued her journey. She thought that she could hear her son crying in the woods. Laque had been on the trail only a short time when she felt a clawing and scratching on her back. Her blanket was torn from her shoulders, and the back of her doeskin dress was ripped.

Laque removed the papoose from her back and found that the fancy clothing with the glistening gems was gone, and, instead of an infant, a young alligator returned her stare. She pushed the alligator away and fell to the ground exhausted, confused, and nearly unconscious. Laque came to her senses in the middle of night. By the light of the moon and the stars, she returned to the shore of Green Lake and called out for her son. In despair, the broken-hearted woman cried out until daybreak.

She climbed to one of the highest elevations around the lake and looked down into the ravine below; she considered leaping into the chasm and taking her own life. As she asked for the forgiveness of the Great Spirit, she heard a voice say "live." She trudged along the path back to her village. She entered her lodge and tearfully told her husband what had happened. He replied that it was obviously the work of an evil spirit. They visited the village's medicine man, the oracle of their nation, to ask what they should do. He told them to return in three days for his answer.

The oracle told them that their child had been taken by the Evil Spirit, "O-nee-hoo-hugh-noo," who had assumed the form of a beautiful woman. However, the Great Spirit has heard the cry of their son and has taken away the power of the wicked spirit. Furthermore, the oracle told them that their infant would be safe and would not be injured in any way. He told them to go up upon a high bank nearby if they wanted to hear their son. The medicine man told them that they would never get him back, but that he would be happy with the Great Spirit.

He also told them that the Good Spirit, "Ha-wah-ne-u," had asked that they give an offering of tobacco each year to ensure the guardian's care of their child. He told them to stand on a high ledge above Green Lake and to cast tobacco into the clear waters below. He said that the first time that they did this, the wicked spirit in the form of a serpent would be driven away and that they would be bothered no more. When they climbed up to the ledge, they saw a huge monster, about 60-foot long, in a threatening pose. The serpent raised his head above the surface of the water and spewed fire and smoke toward them. However, they were too far away to be threatened by the monster.

The couple threw into the lake a large amount of tobacco that spread over a broad expanse of its surface. The color of the lake took on a green hue, and the serpent disappeared. The Great Spirit had broken the spell of the Evil Spirit and had banished the monster forever. Laque and her husband offered tobacco every year. The Onondaga name for the lake, Kai-yah-koo, which means "satisfied with tobacco," is derived from this ceremony. The custom was still being observed when the first White men entered the region.

The Legend of the Origin of Wampum
A young Onondaga man walking through the forest saw a huge bird covered with a heavy coating of wampum. He ran home to his village and told the chief and the people of his village what he had seen. They thought that the bird came from another world, and the Chief offered the hand of his daughter in marriage to the brave who could capture it, dead or alive.

Armed with bows and arrows, the young men of the village went to the "tree of promise" and shot at the enormous bird. Some of the arrows barely scraped the wampum covering the bird. As the arrows caused large amounts of wampum to fall to the ground, new wampum—like Hydra's heads—was created. None of the warriors was able to kill the bird or to wound it so that it would have to come down to earth.

A small boy from a neighboring tribe came to see the wondrous bird that everyone was discussing. His tribe was at war with those who were attempting to bring the bird down. They did not allow him to shoot at the bird; in fact, they threatened him with death if he did. Finally, their chief said, "He is a mere boy; let him shoot on equal terms with you who are brave and fearless warriors." The boy, displaying more skill with the bow and arrow than the mature men, brought the target to the ground with one shot.

The boy received the hand of the chief's daughter in marriage, the wampum was split evenly between the two tribes, and peace was declared between them. The new husband declared that wampum should from then on be the price of blood and peace, and that all thoughts of vengeance should be set aside. This declaration was adopted by all nations of the Iroquois Confederacy. This was the origin of the custom of giving belts of wampum for reasons of hospitality, satisfaction of violated honor, and the encouragement of peace between nations.

The Legend of the Blue Waters

As told in an Onondaga Skaneateles Lake legend, the hills were split apart when the waters of a major flood subsided, which allowed drainage toward the sea. The Six Nations of the Iroquois Confederacy believed that the Great Spirit, the "Invisible Hand," had drained Genesee country of its water, except for the water in the Finger Lakes.

Skaneateles is the bluest of the Finger Lakes, and, according to legend, the sky spirits used to lean out of their home to admire themselves in the mirror of the lake when the heavens were nearer to the lake than they are now. The lake spirits fell in love with the sky spirits and the water absorbed the color of their robes, thus giving the lake its beautiful color.

Joseph Jacobs Museum, Tuscarora Reservation

CHAPTER 4

THE TUSCARORA NATION

"The Tuscaroras were then initiated [into the Iroquois Confederacy in 1722] without enlarging the framework of the Confederacy and formation of the League, by allowing them their own sachems and chiefs, which they took as hereditary from their nation in the South, except on which they gave, as the Holder of the Tree, to sit and enjoy a nominal equality in the councils of the League, by the courtesy of the other five nations. They were not dependent, but were admitted to as full an equality as could be granted them without enlarging the framework of the Confederacy."

Elias Johnson, *History of the Tuscarora Indians*

HISTORY

Eighteenth Century

The Tuscaroras moved northward after their defeat in the Tuscarora Wars in North Carolina in 1711-1713. However, they were not formally accepted as the sixth nation in the Iroquois Confederacy until late 1722. Conditions in North Carolina that the Tuscaroras escaped by migrating to the North were grim. White settlers in North Carolina were not really governed; the little discipline imposed on them came from distant England. Whites encroached on Tuscarora lands without any consideration for property lines or land titles.

Whites and their Indian allies captured Tuscarora men, women, and children and sold them into slavery. The Tuscarora leader, Chief Hancock, retaliated by capturing an expedition of Swiss and Palatine settlers passing through their lands. They executed one of the leaders, John Lawson, who had sold Tuscarora land to which he did not have title. Later, Tuscarora warriors and their Indian allies attacked Whites who had settled on the Pamlico and Trent Rivers.

Governor Edward Hyde of North Carolina, who did not have militia to fight the Tuscaroras, asked for help from Virginia and South Carolina. South Carolina sent Colonel John Barnwell, who defeated the Tuscaroras in 1711 and forced them to sign a peace treaty. The following year, the Tuscaroras resumed the war by attacking settlers along the Neuse, Pamlico, and Trent Rivers. Colonel James Moore of South Carolina retaliated, causing the death and capture of 950 Tuscarora men, women, and children.

Finally, Tom Blount, chief of the Tuscaroras in northern North Carolina and southern Virginia, betrayed Chief Hancock by capturing him and turning him over to the Whites, who executed him. Chief Hancock's followers began their migration to Iroquois country in New York State. Initially, 500 Tuscarora families made the trek northward. They settled on Oneida land between the Unadilla and Chenango Rivers in a village located between the Onondaga and Oneida villages. Some Tuscaroras settled south of Oquaga on the Susquehanna River in New York State as well as along the Juniata and Susquehanna Rivers in Pennsylvania. In 1736, 250 families lived in the Tuscarora village six miles west of Oneida. Another 160 Tuscaroras moved northward from North Carolina in 1766.

Tuscaroras, like other Iroquois nations, attempted to remain neutral and to play the British off against the French and the French against the British. They trapped and hunted as they had in North Carolina and raised crops. Although they were close friends with the Onondagas, Tuscaroras were closest with the Oneidas, on whose land they lived. They were influenced by Rev. Samuel Kirkland, who also had a strong influence on the Oneidas.

Early in the Revolutionary War, Tuscaroras attempted not to take sides. However, in 1776, they could no longer remain neutral. Most Tuscaroras fought in support of the Americans. In August 1779, men of General James Clinton's expedition burned three Tuscarora villages south of Oquaga on the Susquehanna River. In June 1780, Iroquois allies of Sir John Johnson persuaded Tuscaroras and Oneidas living at Ganahsaraga to move to Niagara. In late June that year, Mohawk Chief Joseph Brant burned the remaining Oneida and Tuscarora villages near Oneida Lake. Most Oneidas and Tuscaroras who had been living there also moved to Niagara. By 1780, most Tuscaroras had left the region to which they had moved from North Carolina.

After the Revolutionary War, 130 Tuscaroras, along with Iroquois who had fought on the British side, moved to the Grand River Reservation in Canada. In 1790, over 200 Tuscaroras lived near Big Tree (now Geneseo) on the Genesee River. Subsequently, they moved to Niagara Landing. At this time, 400 Tuscaroras lived in New York State, but only 50-60 lived near Oneida Lake in central New York.

In 1797 at the Treaty of Big Tree, Senecas sold most of their land to Robert Morris who resold it to the Holland Land Company. Two square miles near Lockport were given to the Tuscaroras, who moved there from Niagara Landing. A year later, they were granted an additional square mile, increasing the original Tuscarora Reservation to three square miles, or 1,920 acres.

Nineteenth Century

In 1802, Tuscaroras received $13,722 from the North Carolina Legislature to lease their lands there. In 1804, General Dearborn, Secretary of War, was authorized by Congress to use that money to buy 4,329 acres for the Tuscaroras from the Holland Company, increasing their reservation to 6,249 acres. Some of the remaining

Tuscaroras living in North Carolina moved to the reservation west of Lockport at that time. During the War of 1812, the British burned the Tuscarora village on the reservation. In 1831, the Tuscaroras were paid $3,250 by the North Carolina legislature from the sale of the leased lands.

As with other Iroquois Nations in the first half of the 19th century, the Tuscaroras no longer depended upon hunting but switched to farming for their food. During this time, missionaries living among the Tuscaroras considered them the most self-sufficient and the most successful Iroquois nation in agriculture.

In 1820, due to religious differences between Christians and followers of the New Religion of Handsome Lake, 70 more Tuscaroras moved to Canada. Handsome Lake had not preached to the Tuscaroras; they learned his religion at meetings of the Iroquois Confederacy councils at Buffalo Creek.

In 1838, the Iroquois signed a questionable treaty to sell all their land in New York State and move west of the Mississippi River. A new treaty was negotiated four years later in which the Buffalo Creek and Tonawanda Reservations were sold but the Allegany, Cattaraugus, and Tuscarora Reservations were retained. In 1846, 40 Tuscaroras, many of whom were Baptists, in a party of 200 Iroquois moved to Kansas Territory. Many died in Kansas; the survivors returned to New York State the following year.

During the last half of the 19th century, Tuscaroras became more assimilated into the surrounding White community. In 1890, 400 Tuscaroras lived on the reservation, along with 41 Onondagas and 19 other Iroquois; 4,200 acres of the reservation were under cultivation.

LEGENDS

The Flying Heads

The nations of the Iroquois Confederacy were terrified by the Flying Heads, or "Ko-nea-raw-neh," which had long, flaming hair and always appeared with the wind. These repulsive-looking heads were enormous when in motion, but were about the size of the head of a bear when on land or in the trees. Some medicine men viewed them as bad spirits, and others thought that their coming foretold terrible calamities. Arrows bounced off them, and everyone fled in terror when they appeared. The Flying Heads would go away for months at a time, and the Iroquois would hope that they had left forever. Unfortunately, they always returned.

One evening as the sun was going down, a young Tuscarora woman, De-wan-do, with her baby wrapped in a blanket and slung across her shoulders, was paddling her canoe across a wide river. As she approached the shore, a large visage with flaming hair rose from the water, causing steam to appear above the surface of the river. She was familiar with the Flying Heads, so she ran with her infant into the forest, where she knew that game from the previous day's hunt had been stored. She picked up several pieces of venison, which she threw to the Flying Head, one piece at a time, to slow him down. He stopped to eat each time she threw a piece of meat at him, but eventually she ran out of venison.

De-wan-do threw her blanket at the Flying Head; he ripped it to shreds. She then threw her dress made of doeskin, her leggings, and her moccasins at him as she fled. She was cut and bleeding as she ran unclothed through the brush and briars. Finally, she remembered that an infant's moccasin could be used as a charm to ward off danger. She removed the moccasin from one of her child's feet and flung it at the Flying Head. He stopped, attempted to avoid the moccasin, reeled out of control, and fell to the ground.

De-wan-do ran into the darkest part of the forest, where she climbed a tall pine tree and hid in the branches. Not realizing where she was, the Flying head caught up with her and fell asleep at the base of the tree. De-wan-do climbed down from the tree but accidentally knocked a large limb down on the Flying Head. He was temporarily entangled in the branch but pulled himself clear to pursue De-wan-do. His flaming hair set fire to the brush that he passed through while chasing his quarry back to her longhouse.

Famished, De-wan-do roasted some acorns at the hearth, while her child slept by the fire. She did not realize that the Flying Head had entered her lodge and was watching over her shoulder when she removed the acorns from the fire and ate them. He was surprised by what he saw, because he thought that she was eating hot coals from the fire. He thought, "They must be good. I'll have my share." He gobbled many of the hot coals, screamed in pain, and fled into the woods. A great blaze of fire followed him. That Flying Head never returned to harass the village.

The Stone Giants

In the north country lived a race of giants who subsisted on fish and raw meat. They taught their young boys to rub sand on their bodies until the worn skin bled. Eventually, the skin became calloused and hardened, and when they reached manhood their skin was as hard as rawhide. Some of the sand stuck to the skin and gave them the appearance of stone men.

The giants became more savage and warlike and began to eat the flesh of men. They threatened the Onondagas and Tuscaroras to the south of them. All tribes feared them, because arrows could not pierce their stony skin. They became haughty and overbearing; they mocked the Great Spirit, boasting: "We have created ourselves," and "We are as great as the Great Ruler."

The stone giants scattered the villages of the Six Nations of the Iroquois Confederacy. The giants hid in caves during the daytime and captured and devoured men, women, and children at night. The Iroquois appealed repeatedly to the Great Spirit, but their villages continued to be attacked. Iroquois warriors shot their sturdiest arrows with the sharpest flint tips at the giants, but the arrows snapped and the flint crumbled when they struck the stone coats. Then they became food for the cannibals.

Eventually, the Great Spirit realized that if he did not take action, the Iroquois Confederacy would no longer exist. He directed the Holder of the Heavens to go down to earth and exterminate the race of stone giants. The Holder of the Heavens hid in the forest, took on the form of a stone giant, and went out among them. He impressed them with his overpowering strength and was appointed their great Chief. He waved his war club in the air and, speaking of the Tuscaroras, said: "Now is the time to destroy these puny men and have a feast as never before." He commanded the stone giants to hide in the caves on the side of the hill whose crest contained the Tuscarora palisade.

After directing the stone giants to attack at dawn, the Holder of the Heavens went to the top of the hill and shook the entire world. Rocks were cast loose, landslides covered the caves, and new hills and valleys were created. All but one of the stone giants were crushed. The lone survivor ran out of his partially collapsed cave with a yell and did not stop running until he reached the Allegheny mountains to the south. He cowered there in a large cave. The

Tuscaroras sustained no injuries and went about their business as they did before the arrival of the stone giants.

The Hunter and Medicine Legend

A great Tuscarora hunter was a generous man who supplied not only his own family with food but also provided game to his friends and neighbors. Because birds and animals of the forest also benefited from his generosity, he was known as the "Protector of birds and animals."

He was an expert hunter who became a brave warrior when the Tuscaroras were on the warpath. In one battle, he had killed many of his enemies and was looking at the dead all around him. In an unguarded moment, he received a savage tomahawk blow to the head from the only adversary left on the field. The enemy warrior scalped him and ran away. His fellow Tuscaroras saw what had happened and, thinking him to be dead, left the field.

A fox, who had benefited from his generosity, saw him lying on the field of battle and immediately began to think of means of restoring him to life. The fox, hoping that one of his friends might know of a medicine to heal the hunter's wounds and bring him back to life, returned to the forest and uttered the "death lament" to call his friends together. Hundreds of birds and animals gathered around the hunter and asked the fox what had happened. He described finding the hunter who appeared to be dead.

The bear spoke before the grand council of animals to ask if anyone knew of a medicine that might restore the hunter's life. When it was realized that none of the animals had such a medicine, they howled a mournful requiem for the dead. An oriole attracted by the council asked about the cause of their lamentations. The oriole flew away to ask all of his friends, including the eagles, if they knew of an appropriate medicine.

The combined council of birds and animals decided that the only way to restore the hunter to life would be to find his scalp. The fox's search for the scalp failed; the pigeon hawk and the white heron also tried to find it without success. Finally, the crow, having volunteered to search for the scalp, flew over a village where he saw it stretched out to dry. The crow snatched the scalp and returned it to the united council. They attempted to fit it to the hunter's head, but it had dried out too much. They looked around unsuccessfully for something to moisten the scalp.

The great eagle had a suggestion: "My wings are never furled: night and day, for years and hundreds of years, the dews of heaven have been collected upon my back as I sat in my nest above the clouds. Perhaps these waters may have a virtue no earthly fountain can possess, we will see." Then the great eagle plucked a feather from her wing, dipped it into the moist elixir, and applied it to the scalp, which became pliable. The scalp could now be fitted to the hunter's head; nevertheless, the birds and animals wondered how they could make the it adhere to the skull to restore life.

Members of the council searched and brought back rare bark, flowers, and leaves to mix with the brains of birds and the flesh of animals to form a healing potion. They mixed the potion with dew and applied it to the scalp. The hunter immediately look up surprised, wondering how he came to be in the middle of this large gathering of birds and animals. They explained to the hunter how they had found him and their desire to return him to life because of all of the kind things he had done for them.

The birds and animals gave the hunter the elixir that had restored his life and told him: "It was the gift of the Great Spirit to man. He alone had directed them in the affairs of the council, had brought the eagle to furnish the heavenly moisture, and had given them the wisdom to make the preparation to furnish the man with a medicine that should be effective for every wound." The birds and animals all returned to their habitats, happy about their great accomplishment. The hunter returned home and told his tribe about the wonderful elixir that had returned him to life. According to legend, the medicine is used to this day by Tuscaroras who are favored by the Great Spirit.

The Legend of Ro-qua-ho

The Tuscaroras were bothered by a multi-colored lizard, Ro-qua-ho, a fast runner that struck heavy blows with its tail. Ro-qua-ho hid from the warriors and killed them as they walked down the trail. One day, a party of four Tuscarora hunters walked by a large hollow tree and noticed many large claw marks on its trunk. They thought that the claw marks had been made by a bear. One of the braves climbed the tree and pounded on the trunk to make the tree's inhabitant to come out of its abode.

The braves were terrified to see Ro-qua-ho come out of the tree. The three warriors on the ground ran for their lives but were caught by the feared lizard, killed, and dragged back to the hollow tree. The brave in the tree jumped down and began to run. He stopped and turned around when he heard someone calling to him. A dignified man with a long flowing beard said, "Why run? I have seen the distress of my people, and I have come to deliver them out of trouble; now confide in me, and we will prevail. I am your bene-factor, Tarenyawagon. Get behind me, the enemy is approaching."

In an instant, this Celestial Being was changed into a large white bear. The struggle with Ro-qua-ho was fierce, but the great white bear and the man killed the variegated lizard. The Tuscaroras were relieved to have a serious threat to their well-being removed.

The Legend of the Mosquito

According to Tuscarora legend, the area around their principal village used to be infested with mosquitoes. Shodiosko, the "Mischief Maker," destroyed the mosquitoes by building a large smudge fire into which he threw sacred incense. The mosquitoes saw the column of smoke and combined into one huge mosquito to avoid extinction.

Shodiosko, seeing that both the fire and the mosquito were larger than he could control, leapt into the column of smoke and was elevated to the sky. He hoped that the sacred incense would help him to mend his wicked ways.

The enormous mosquito flew close to Shodiosko's village, and the Great Spirit was concerned for the well-being of the people. He directed a large bird to sweep down from the heavens to capture and kill the mosquito. As the bird was flying away with the body of the mosquito, one of the mosquito's legs fell toward the earth. A young man shot an arrow that pierced the leg. As blood flowed from the wound, each drop became a potential mosquito. However, the mosquitoes created from the blood were driven away by the smudge fire. This is the Indian explanation of why the Tuscaroras did not have a problem with mosquitoes; they flew to other areas to avoid the "big smoke."

Shako:wi Cultural Center, Oneida

Stained Glass Window, Shak:wi Cultural Center, Oneida
(Great White Pine Tree of Peace and Wolf, Turtle, and Bear Clan)

CHAPTER 5

THE ONEIDA NATION

"The Oneidas are thought to have been the most susceptible to religious instruction. The Mohawks, although more warlike, were also ever ready to listen to the teachings of the missionaries sent to them from time to time. As a nation, however, the Oneidas were the most resorted to for advice in negotiations with the Confederacy to win them to prepare the minds of the remaining cantons. And for their naturally mild, peaceable dispositions and good counsel they were doubtless termed 'wise in counsel.'"

J. K. Bloomfield, *The Oneidas*

HISTORY

Seventeenth Century

The home region of the Oneida Nation was near Oneida Creek, which flows into Oneida Lake. Oneidas controlled the area around Wood Creek and the upper Mohawk Valley. The region in which they hunted extended northward to the St. Lawrence River and southward toward the Susquehanna River. The principal Oneida village, as described by Dutch journalist Harmen van den Bogaert in 1634, was near Munnsville in Madison County. Thirty years later it was located 15 miles from Oneida Lake. In 1696, the village was burned by the French.

Oneidas, like other Iroquois nations, were active in the fur trade. Beaver pelts were used to trade for European tools and materials. In the fur trade, the Algonquins and Hurons were allied with the French, and the Iroquois were allied with the Dutch and, later, the British. Oneida war parties ventured to the north, the west, and the south in search of pelts. Loss of warriors was critical to the Oneidas because they were a small nation. Losses were compensated by adopting captured Algonquins and Hurons, who were assimilated into the Oneida Nation, as were some Mohawk warriors. The Oneida leader Shenandoah was an adopted Susquehannock.

Eighteenth Century

In 1757, the main Oneida village was located six miles from Oneida Lake. A new village called Canowaroghere was built in 1762. Some Oneida and Mohawk families lived at Oquaga (later Windsor) on the Susquehanna River. Following the Tuscarora Wars of 1711-1713 in North Carolina, many Tuscaroras moved from North Carolina to live on Oneida land.

In 1767, Samuel Kirkland, a Presbyterian minister, established a missionary church with the Oneida Nation. Rev. Kirkland was a disciple of Jonathan Edwards, a fundamentalist who stressed self-discipline and determinism. Edwards emphasized the individual, who was asked to repent and to accept Jesus Christ in order to be saved. Because most of Kirkland's followers were warriors, the status of chiefs was weakened.

During the French and Indian Wars, Oneidas attempted to

remain neutral. Nevertheless, they were drawn into the war on the side of the British. In the 1760s, the Oneida Nation experienced food shortages, disputes among factions within the nation, and encroachment of their lands by Whites. Rev. Kirkland seemed to have arrived at their time of need.

Leading up to the Revolutionary War, Oneidas were pulled in two directions: Rev. Kirkland sided with the Colonials, and Sir William Johnson, the Crown's Commissioner of Indian Affairs, was obviously allied with the British. Also, the Presbyterianism of Rev. Kirkland was pitted against Johnson's Anglicanism. Nations of the Iroquois Confederacy were divided between backing the Colonials and supporting the British. Attempts at reconciliation among the Six Nations failed.

Finally, the council fire maintained by the Onondagas for the Iroquois Confederacy was extinguished, allowing each nation to pursue its own course. Oneidas and their brothers, the Tuscaroras, were pro-American, and the other four nations of the Confederacy were pro-British because of past alliances. A few of the Oneida chiefs were pro-British. The Oneidas were spared raids by Major General John Sullivan similar to those made on the Seneca, Cayuga, and Onondaga communities. Oneida warriors fought bravely alongside Colonials at the Battle of Oriskany in 1777 and, two years later, helped to provision Washington's struggling, starving army.

Late in the Revolutionary War, some Oneidas moved to Niagara. Their villages around Oneida Lake were destroyed, and the remnants of their populace moved to Schenectady, where they suffered from cold and starvation. After the war, Oneidas were scattered across the state, their crops burned, their villages leveled, and the other nations of the Confederacy, except for the Tuscaroras, turned away from them. The Oneida Nation paid a heavy price for its pro-American loyalties.

Oneidas who returned to the Oneida Lake area after the war were involved in disputes, some of which were between those who had been pro-American and others who had been pro-British during the war. Oneida land continued to be encroached upon by Whites. In 1788, a land company sponsored by John Livingston persuaded the Oneidas to lease most of their land for 999 years, which was not allowed by the New York State Constitution. New

York State wanted to buy land for settlers from the Oneidas.

New York State and the Federal Government appreciated the Oneida's suffering and support during the Revolutionary War. Finally in 1784, the Continental Congress granted Oneida claims to almost six million acres of land by the Treaty of Fort Stanwix. This guarantee was renewed in the treaties of Fort Harmar (1789), Canandaigua (1784), and Oneida (1794).

In the last treaty, the U.S. Government compensated Oneidas for their contributions during the Revolutionary War by paying them $5,000 and building a church, a gristmill, and a sawmill. Also, they shared a $4,500 annuity with the other Iroquois nations. In 1785, Oneidas sold to New York State the land that is now Broome and Chenango Counties for $15,500. Three years later, they set aside 300,000 acres in Madison and Oneida counties for their own use.

Nineteenth Century

Discord between the two factions of the Oneida Nation that had existed during the Revolutionary War intensified in the early 1800s. Chief Shenandoah led those who were pro-American during the war, Christians, and in favor of accommodation with Whites. Chief Cornelius led others who were pro-British during the war, believed in the Religion of the Longhouse, and did not want contact with Whites. In 1805, the differences were so profound that the factions settled in separate reservations near Oneida Lake.

During the 19th century, Oneidas had less territory on which to hunt because of their land sales. White settlers continued to encroach on their lands and influenced them by introducing White culture. Neighboring Whites encouraged the Oneidas to become farmers, to become Christians (most Oneidas were, at least nominally), and to send their children to White schools. Whites also favored a male-dominated family in place of the matrilineal society of the Iroquois.

Two Oneida leaders died early in the 1800s: Rev. Kirkland in 1808 and Chief Shenandoah in 1816. The Christian community had been shrinking until 1816, when Episcopal lay-reader Eleazar Williams came to live with the Oneidas. He was a fervent Christian, an accomplished speaker, and a good communicator who spoke the Oneida language. He immediately obtained the support of the Chief

Shenandoah faction and worked to gain the favor of followers of Chief Cornelius.

Williams proposed that the Oneidas move to Wisconsin, where they would be less influenced by White culture. Oneida chiefs opposed the relocation, but Williams promoted the move by securing 500,000 acres, subsequently reduced to 65,426 acres, from the Menominees. In 1823, some Oneidas moved to Wisconsin, west of Green Bay. Williams wanted to establish a religious empire to lead. The Ogden Land Company supported the move because it had pre-emptive rights to buy the land in New York State from the Oneidas.

Oneidas who moved to Wisconsin settled in two communities: an Anglican and a Methodist settlement. The New Religion of Handsome Lake was not practiced at Green Bay. By 1860, lumber companies had stripped the forests, encouraging settlers in the region to farm the land. Oneidas were pressured to sell their land to lumber barons and to area farmers. Lobbyists wanted to move the Oneida Nation farther west.

In 1838, the Treaty of Buffalo Creek proposed the relocation of all New York State Iroquois, including the Oneidas, to Kansas Territory. The Oneidas did not want to move to Kansas. Some wanted to stay in New York State, some wanted to move to Ontario, Canada, and others wanted to move but did not have a destination in mind. In 1839, 242 Oneidas sold their land in New York and purchased 5,200 acres of land near London, Ontario. During the next decade, 410 Oneidas moved to Ontario; only 200 Oneidas remained in New York, either on what was left of their land or on the Onondaga Reservation south of Syracuse.

Oneidas who moved to London, Ontario, politically joined with the chiefs from the much larger Six Nations Reservation to the east. Farming was the principal industry, supplemented by lumbering during the winter. Surplus crops were sold for income; additional income was earned from the sale of baskets and cornhusk mats. Some Oneidas worked in the flax and tobacco fields.

LEGENDS

The Legend of the Oneida Stone

The boundary between the Onondagas and the Oneidas was marked by Deep Spring, "De-o-song-wa," a resting place on the Great Central Trail of the Iroquois that extended 240 miles from Albany to Buffalo. South of Deep Spring, the boundary line of Oneida country crossed the Susquehanna River at its confluence with the Chenango River and continued into Pennsylvania. North of Deep Spring, the boundary line bent westward so that Oneida territory encompassed Oneida Lake.

A large, round-shaped stone near Deep Spring was unlike any other stone in the vicinity. Oneidas used the stone as their sacrificial altar and called it "Onia," the Oneida word for stone. The Oneidas were called "Onionta-aug, people of the stone" or "Who springs from the stone." All Oneida Nation councils as well as festivals and religious activities were held around the stone.

Eventually, the Oneidas moved from their location along the Oneida River to where Oneida Creek flows into Oneida Lake. According to legend, the Oneida Stone, without human intervention, followed them to their new village. Next, they moved the council fire to the top of a hill west of Oneida Creek. Again, the Oneida Stone followed them to the site of their new village in a butternut grove overlooking beautiful countryside.

The wise and powerful chiefs of the Oneida Nation met regularly around the Oneida Stone as the nation grew and prospered. The eloquence of Oneida sachems could be heard from the location of the stone. Chief Shenandoah was one the speakers to expound wisdom from this site. The principal activities at the stone were sacred rites at the time of the harvest moon and the new year.

In 1850, the Oneida Stone was moved from Madison County to Forest Hill Cemetery in Utica, where space was reserved around the stone for future Oneida burials. About 200 Oneidas and Onondagas attended ceremonies at the cemetery and kissed the stone. Speeches were made by chiefs of the Oneida and Onondaga Nations; they affirmed their agreement with the new location of the stone. The Oneida Stone was located in Forest Hill Cemetery for over a century. Subsequently, it was moved to Oneida territory near Oneida.

The Sacrifice of Aliquipiso

An Oneida village was raided by a band of Mingoes from the North. The Mingoes had listened to bad spirits, and they had killed everyone and had destroyed everything in their path. Oneida women and children abandoned their lodges and fled to the large rocks in the hills, where their men protected them. The savage marauders searched for days without success for the people of the village.

The Oneidas ran out of food; however, they feared that if they foraged and hunted, they would be killed. Meeting in council, the chiefs could think of no solution to their problems. If they remained behind the rocks on the cliff, they would starve; if they ventured out, they would be enslaved or brutally murdered.

A young maiden, Aliquipiso, visited the council of sachems and told them about an idea that the Good Spirits had given to her. They told her that if the rocks high on the cliff were rolled into the valley below, everything there would be destroyed. The Good Spirits also told Aliquipiso that if she would lure the plundering Mingoes to the valley below the rocks, they would be killed also. The chiefs were relieved to hear of a solution to their troubles. They gave her a necklace of white wampum, made her a princess of the Oneida Nation, and reminded her that she was loved by the Great Spirit.

Aliquipiso left her people in the middle of the night and climbed down from the cliff. The next morning, Mingo scouts found a young maiden wandering around lost in the forest. They led Aliquipiso back to the abandoned Oneida village, where they attempted to get her to reveal the hiding place of the Oneidas. They tortured her; she held out for a long time and won the respect of her captors. Finally, she told the Mingoes that she would lead them to her people. When darkness came, Aliquipiso led her captors to the base of the cliff. Two strong Mingoes held her in their grasp and were prepared to take her life at the first hint of deception.

The Mingo warriors gathered around Aliquipiso, thinking that she was going to show them an opening into a large cave in the cliff. Suddenly, she lifted her head and let out a piercing cry—a forewarning of death. Above them, the starving Oneidas pushed the large boulders over the cliff. The Mingoes did not have time to get out the way and were crushed under the large rocks, along with the

79

Oneida heroine.

Aliquipiso, who was buried near the scene of her courageous sacrifice, was mourned by the Oneidas for many moons. The Great Spirit used her hair to create woodbine, called "running hairs" by the Iroquois, the climbing vine that protects old trees. The Great Spirit changed her body into honeysuckle, which was called "the blood of brave women" by Oneidas.

The Legend of the Peace Queen

A Iroquois maiden known for her good judgment was chosen to act as a judge in settling disputes for nations of the Iroquois Confederation. They provided her with a lodge deep in the forest and called her Genetaska, "the Peace Queen." Iroquois women considered her a sacred being. Her word was law and could not be contested.

One afternoon while hunting in the woods, an Oneida hunter killed a buck with an arrow through the heart. As he was removing the skin from the deer and was about to cut it into quarters, an Onondaga hunter stepped out from the trees and said that the kill belonged to him. He claimed that he had fatally wounded the buck before the Oneida shot his arrow to finish him off. Their argument became heated, and they fought for several hours without either gaining advantage over the other.

Finally, the exhausted young men decided to present their disagreement to the Peace Queen for resolution. She scolded them for fighting within her domain, directed them to divide the deer equally, and told them to return to their villages. However, the Onondaga brave was smitten with the beauty of the Peace Queen and did not want to return to his home. He proposed to her and asked her to share his lodge. She told him that she could not marry because of her sacred duty to the Iroquois Confederacy. The saddened Onondaga hunter prepared to return to his village.

The Oneida hunter also had fallen in love with the Peace Queen. She refused his offer of marriage as well, but she responded so softly and affectionately that he could not get her out of his mind. She asked the two young men to leave in peace. They were reconciled and became friends with the common bond of unrequited love for the same woman.

However, Genetaska thought about the young Oneida all the

time—upon waking, during the day, and while going to sleep in the evening. Many moons passed, and the Peace Queen fulfilled her obligation to the Iroquois to settle disputes. However, her heart was saddened with longing for the brave, gentle Oneida warrior.

One day she pined for him as she warmed herself by the fire, and he appeared before her. He looked pale and haggard and explained that he could not live without her. He had lost interest in the hunt, and he no longer enjoyed playing lacrosse and other games with his friends. He admitted that the light had gone out of his life, and he asked again for her hand in marriage. This time, she agreed to become his wife. She regretted walking away from her sacred obligations, but she knew that she would wither away if she did not marry the one whom she loved. She and her intended traveled to their new home.

The chiefs who had elected her Peace Queen to settle disputes were angry with her for abandoning her responsibilities. They tore down her lodge in the woods and abolished the position of Peace Queen. As might be expected, arguments and fights resumed within the Iroquois Confederacy.

Iroquois Indian Museum, Howe's Cave

Statue of Kateri Tekakwitha, Auriesville

CHAPTER 6

THE MOHAWK NATION

"Fighting, fierce and furious, conquest and revenge, hunting and man huntings were both business and recreation to the early denizens of the Mohawk Valley.... The inhabitants of the Mohawk Valley at the earliest time of which we have accurate records, the people who made it famous, whose residence there was of such importance in the history and development of North America, were called Ga-ne-ga-o-no in their own language, Caniegas by the French, and Mohawks by the English."

T. Wood Clarke, *The Bloody Mohawk*

HISTORY

Seventeenth Century

The Mohawk Nation was the Keeper of the Eastern door of the Iroquois Confederacy. As the Iroquois nation closest to Albany and early Dutch fur traders, who gave them tools and weapons, they were respected by other Iroquois nations. Also, they were highly regarded as warriors by enemy nations, such as the Hurons to the north. The home region of the Mohawks extended from Schoharie Creek, west of Amsterdam, to east of Little Falls. Their hunting territory stretched from the Adirondack Mountains in the north to the East Branch of the Susquehanna River near Oneonta to the south.

Mohawks had at least three villages, all on the south side of the Mohawk River:

- Ossernenon, also called Lower or First Castle, was located near Auriesville. Later, it was moved westward and called Caughnawaga. After its destruction by the French general de Tracy's expedition in 1666, it was rebuilt north of the Mohawk River on the west side of Cayadutta Creek near Fonda. In 1668, many captured Hurons and Algonquins lived in the village. It retained the name Caughnawaga, which was also the name given to a village established by Mohawks and Oneidas from the Mohawk Valley at La Prairie on the Island of Montreal in 1676.
- Kanagaro, also called Second Castle, was located six miles from Caughnawaga. It was burned by the French in 1666 and was moved north of the Mohawk River.
- Tionnontoguen, the Upper Castle, was the largest Mohawk village and was the "capital" of Mohawk country.

Because they were the easternmost of the Iroquois nations, Mohawks were the first influenced by settlers of the Eastern seaboard, particularly the Dutch. They provided furs to the Dutch in return for knives, swords, and axes like those that the French were providing to enemies of the Iroquois, the Algonquins and Montagnais. Mahicans were located in the Albany area; Mohawks were permitted to cross their territory to trade with the Dutch.

Mohawks fought with their Algonquin neighbors to the north to confiscate European tools and weapons and to obtain additional beaver pelts to trade. In the early 1640s, Mohawks obtained firearms from the British and the Dutch, which changed the methods of warfare dramatically. Mohawks excelled in fighting with their newly acquired weapons and added to their previous reputation as feared warriors. In 1653, Mohawks signed a peace treaty with the French; however, they continued to fight with Indian allies of the French. Many Mohawks opposed this uncertain peace.

In 1664, New York became a British colony. Mohawks continued to trade with the Dutch in Albany, even though it was now under the British flag. Dutch goods were usually of higher quality than French goods and cost less. In 1665, the French general de Courcelle arrived to attack the Mohawks but was ambushed by them and retreated. The following year, General de Tracy accomplished what his countryman had failed to do—destroy the Mohawk villages. In 1667, Mohawks and other Iroquois nations signed a peace treaty with the French at Quebec.

When the Mohawks who had settled at La Prairie near Montreal found that the site was too damp to grow corn, some moved upriver to Sault Ste. Louis, near the Lachine Rapids. The new village was called Caughnawaga, the same name as the Mohawk village along the Mohawk River in New York.

Eighteenth Century

Successful French attacks against the Mohawks and the Onondagas late in the 17th century motivated the Iroquois to sign another (short-lived) treaty with the French in 1701. During the 18th century, a series of wars were fought between the British and the French: Queen Anne's war (1702-1713), King George's War (1744-1748), and the French and Indian War (1754-1763). In each war, the British and the French tried to attract Iroquois allies. Iroquois nations attempted to stay neutral, but long-term neutrality in the environment that existed at the time was virtually impossible. It became obvious to both countries that the Iroquois Confederacy was playing one off against the other.

The Mohawk Nation participated in Queen Anne's War by raiding towns in New England, including Deerfield and Groton, Massachusetts. They engaged in the contraband trade between Montreal and Albany (tacitly agreed to by the British and the French) before and after Queen Anne's War. The French convinced many Mohawks to move to their missions in Canada.

Mohawks had two principal villages in the early 18th century, Lower Mohawk Castle (Tiononderoge) near Fort Hunter and Upper Mohawk Castle (Canajoharie). In 1712, Protestant refugees from the Palatinate in Germany settled along Schoharie Creek. Many more refugees settled along the Mohawk River beginning in 1723.

In 1719, in an attempt to keep their Iroquois allies, the British invited four "Indian Kings," three Mohawk chiefs: Theyanoguin, "Chief Hendrick," his brother, Cenelitonoro, and Joseph Brant's grandfather, Sagaynguaroughton; and one Mahican chief to England. They attended banquets, had an audience with the Queen, and had their portraits painted. The Mohawk chiefs asked Queen Anne to send Church of England missionaries to Iroquois villages. She complied, and the following year a chapel was built at Fort Hunter where Schoharie Creek flows into the Mohawk River.

Chief Hendrick had been converted to Protestantism by a Dutch pastor, Godfrey Dellius. Chief Hendrick became a lay preacher among the Mohawks; many Mohawks became Protestants. In 1755, Hendrick was killed in the Battle of Lake George in the French and Indian War, while leading a band of Mohawks in support of Sir William Johnson.

In the 1740s, Iroquois from Caughnawaga moved to the head of Lake St. Francis, between the St. Regis and Racquette Rivers. The move was made for three reasons: the land at Caughnawaga had become less fertile, the French wanted another outpost on the upper St. Lawrence River, and serious family disputes had erupted.

In 1747, the St. Regis Reservation, also called "Akwesasne," was established on the south shore of the upper St. Lawrence River by disgruntled Iroquois from the Caughnawaga settlement. They were pro-French and contributed to the French influence along the river. Part of this reservation was in Canada and part was in the United States, near Ogdensburg.

Because the Mohawks had been allied with the British for years, many fought against the Americans in the Revolutionary War. In 1777, stung by their loss at Oriskany, Colonials and their Oneida allies attacked the Mohawk villages at Fort Hunter and Canajoharie. Many Mohawks from the Fort Hunter settlement joined British General Burgoyne in his attack on New York. Eventually, these Fort Hunter Mohawks settled at Lachine, near Montreal. Their leader was John Deserontyon.

Loyalist Mohawks were understandably reluctant to return to the Mohawk Valley, where Americans held the land that had been guaranteed to the Iroquois by the Treaty of Fort Stanwix in 1768. In 1783, Ontario Provincial Governor Frederick Haldimand offered the Mohawks land near the Bay of Quinté that he had obtained from the Mississauga Indians.

Mohawks from the Upper Castle at Canajoharie, led by Joseph Brant, went to Fort Niagara. Governor Haldimand invited them to come to the Bay of Quinté, but they wanted to be closer to the Senecas and other Iroquois who had settled in western New York State. In 1784, the Governor bought a large tract of land along the Grand River in an attempt to unite the Mohawks. Deserontyon and the Mohawks at Lachine declined his offer to live there because the site was too close to the Americans; they moved to the reservation at the Bay of Quinté, which is called "Tyendinaga" or "Deseronto." Initially, it contained 17,000 acres. Brant and the Mohawks at Fort Niagara moved to the Grand River Reservation.

Nineteenth Century

Indian reservations (reserves) in Canada all had Catholic churches because of the French influence. In the 1840s, Methodist churches were established on some reservations in Canada. The teachings of Handsome Lake faded among the Mohawks during the 19th century but were rekindled during the early 20th century.

During the 19th century, as with other Iroquois nations, hunting for a livelihood declined, while farming increased. In the late 19th century, Mohawks began the high steelwork on construction projects for skyscrapers and bridges for which they became known.

LEGENDS

The Legend of Two Serpents

This Mohawk legend is similar to the Seneca legend, "The Serpent of Bare Hill." The Mohawk Nation faced a severe food shortage: few deer and moose roamed the forest; streams contained virtually no fish; the sky was empty of birds; and crops were sparse and of poor quality. Two young Mohawk hunters traveled east of their usual hunting territory to search for food. They found little until they reached the ocean, which was farther east than they had ever been. Food was bountiful near the ocean.

In the distance, the braves could see something glowing in the water in the direction of the sun in the eastern sky. They paddled their canoe toward the glow and found two small serpents, a gold one that seemed to shimmer and a silver one that appeared to emit light. The young men picked them out of the water and placed them in their canoe. They discontinued their hunt for food, realizing that their fellow Mohawks would be captivated by the snake-like creatures.

The tribe built a cage for the serpents near their village. Many of the villagers, fascinated by the glow, spent hours watching the serpents. The creatures had incredible appetites. They ate everything: meat, fish, vegetables—even grass, roots, and leaves. The tribe, which already had a shortage of food, was cleaned out of edibles. The serpents grew rapidly and caused the Mohawks to build increasingly large cages.

When the food supply ran out, the creatures became angry, broke out of their cages, and attacked the Mohawks. Many people were eaten by the serpents; the rest fled into the woods. The Mohawks attacked the serpents with war clubs, spears, and flint-tipped arrows; however, the creatures had grown too large and were too strong. When they had stripped the area of food, the serpents moved westward. None of the Iroquois nations could subdue them. As they traveled, they fouled the water and destroyed the landscape.

Eventually, the silver serpent moved northward, and the golden one slithered southward. They seemed to enjoy killing as they drank small lakes dry and defoliated the forests. For many years, the Iroquois did not see the serpents; they thought that they had moved out of their region. One day, however, a Mohawk saw the golden snake traveling toward Mohawk territory and was told that the Silver one was headed in their direction also. He hurried home to tell his brothers of the threat.

Mohawks were divided on a course of action: some wanted to stay and fight, many wanted to run, and others wanted to feed the serpents as they had in the past. Fights broke out among the Mohawk Nation, and men were killed. While they were arguing, the serpents attacked with a vengeance, and many people died.

Some escaped to a mountain retreat that they thought was safe. Unfortunately, the serpents knew where they were.

A young Mohawk boy told his elders that he had had an unusual dream, one in which he had learned how to kill the creatures. A willow bow was constructed with a bowstring made from the hair of clan mothers. Special arrows tipped with white flint were made. When the serpents arrived at the hiding place, the young boy shot his special arrows at the serpents. His aim was true; the arrows pierced their skins, and he killed both creatures.

Mohawk elders passed the legend down through the generations that the serpents represented the pain and distress that White men entering their lands would cause them. Furthermore, according to their symbolism, the golden serpent was interpreted as the United States, and the silver one was Canada. In another version of the legend, the principal threats to the Six Nations of the Iroquois were thought to be from within, due to loss of the values of their forefathers, to a decline in spirituality, and to widespread greed.

The Legend of the Peacemaker

Deganawida, the Peacemaker, was a Huron who moved to Iroquois country and became the mentor of Hiawatha while visiting the Onondagas. He left the Huron Nation when he encountered the questioning and doubt faced by all prophets in their own land. After making speeches of peace among the Onondagas, he traveled to Mohawk territory.

The Mohawks were skeptical of his powers and needed a sign before they would believe his message. The Mohawk chiefs decided that Deganawida should climb to the top branch of a tree on a cliff alongside Cohoes Falls, where the Mohawk River flows into the Hudson River. The Mohawks would chop down the tree, dropping it into the rapids. If Deganawida survived, they would accept his message. When the Mohawks returned the next morning, they found Deganawida sitting by his fire.

This cured the Mohawks of their skepticism; they were convinced of Daganawida's powers and believed his message of peace. They became a founder of the League of the Iroquois.

The Legend of the Pipe of Peace

The peace pipe was always smoked at Iroquois councils at which treaties were made. The practice of smoking the pipe of peace was originated years ago by an Iroquois sachem who possessed considerable wisdom and good judgment. He traveled among the tribes of the Iroquois Confederacy promoting peace. He advised them to be charitable and to aid one another. He counseled those who were blessed with plenty to help those who were less fortunate.

This astute sachem attended all councils to settle disputes among tribes and councils of war. His sage advice facilitated peaceful settlements. By providing a good example and by applying sound judgment, he settled disagreements and averted war. Among the nations of the Iroquois Confederacy, he became known as the Peacemaker. When he grew old and frail, he gathered his people around him and told them that he was going to join the Great Spirit in Sky Land. He told them not to be concerned, because he would reappear in another form and continue to be with them forever.

After the death of the wise sachem, one of the chiefs found an unusual plant growing in front of the Peacemaker's lodge. They heard the voice of the Peacemaker saying that this strange plant was the tobacco plant, the form in which he was reappearing to them. He told them to smoke this new plant in pipes made of stone. He also advised that they pass the Pipe of Peace around in their councils in memory of him.

The custom of smoking the Pipe of Peace at all councils was established. The chiefs believed that they could envision the Peacemaker in the smoke that wafted upward from their stone pipes. He had told them always to keep commitments that they made in his presence. The Iroquois never broke a promise accompanied by the passing of the Pipe of Peace.

Iroquois Longhouse at Ganondagan, near Victor

CHAPTER 7

IROQUOIS CULTURE

"At the time the Whites arrived, the most powerful Indians in north-eastern North America were those centered in New York State — various groups who spoke dialects of the Iroquois language.... Their culture is now known to be indigenous and to have emerged from that of the lower Great Lakes several centuries before the arrival of the Whites. They had trained systematically to equip themselves for warfare in the woodlands; they grew in population, in prosperity, and in the complexity of their culture.... Some romantics have called the Iroquois 'The Greeks of America' — but it would probably be more accurate to regard them as our native Prussian Junkers."

Peter Farb, *Man's Rise to Civilization: The Cultural Ascent of the Indians of North America*

The Matrilineal Society of the Iroquois

The Iroquois established in their Constitution of the Ho-dé-no-sau-nee (also Haudenosaunee), People of the Longhouse, that women's rights would always be protected by their laws. Iroquois children were the sons and daughters of the mother's clan; they were not the inheritors of the clan rights of the father. A clan is an element of Native-American society that traces its descent from a common ancestor. If a Seneca woman of the Bear Clan married a Mohawk, their children would be Senecas of the Bear Clan down through the generations. This tribal law maintained the purity of clan descent.

The Iroquois mother was responsible for the care of her children during their infancy and childhood and for the development of their character. The father had little control or authority over his children until his sons matured and became his companions in the hunt and on the warpath. Iroquois women owned property and continued to own it after they married. They could dispose of the property as they chose. By the Iroquois law of descent, children could not inherit property from their father, because they were not of their father's clan. They were inheritors of their mother's clan.

Women arranged all marriages for their children. A woman might consult with the elders of the clan, but the responsibility was hers. Settlement of family disputes was the responsibility of the mother with the advice of other clan members. If her child's marriage had serious problems, the mother decided whether or not the couple should separate. Separations occurred rarely because they were considered a disgrace. If reconciliation was not possible, usually because of incompatibility, a divorce was granted. The divorced wife returned to the lodge of her mother with her children and her property.

When a chief died, a council was called to elect a new chief. The mother of the family in which the death occurred selected the most reliable male of her own line of descent as chief. She might consult with others, but the final decision was her responsibility. If the appointed chief was derelict in his duties or did not measure up to expectations, the mother was responsible for removing him as chief and selecting another male in her line of descent to replace him. Removing a chief was called dehorning because the deer antlers that were the symbol of his chiefhood were taken away.

Iroquois women were appointed to serve in religious feasts with men. Women were also responsible for all burial or death feasts. They were considered the guardians of all plants, particularly the "three sisters": beans, corn, and squash. Women were also the guardians of the "chief" wampum belts that were sent to them by the great councils when a chief was elected. These wampum belts confirmed a nomination of a chief and legalized his election.

Iroquois women had these rights long before pioneer settlers moved into central New York. The first Women's Rights Convention in Seneca Falls on July 19-20, 1848, addressed conditions that are difficult to envision today: under United States law, women were not permitted to vote, to obtain a college education, or to own property, and their wages were turned over to their husbands. In cases of separation and divorce, guardianship was automatically given to the husband. By law, a woman's inheritance went to her husband. She was not entitled to the rights given automatically to men of the lowest station, whether they were born in the United States or were immigrants.

Native-American women had a superior position in society and rights greater than those of the mothers, wives, and daughters of White settlers in the region. However, the Native Americans were thought to be "uncivilized" by pioneer settlers who considered themselves "civilized."

Life in the Longhouse

The Iroquois, People of the Longhouse, lived in a world of luxuriant forests, beautiful lakes, rippling streams, rich soil, and plentiful fish and game. Patterns of their existence were fixed by the sun, rain, snow, and wind. Their life revolved around the seasons. Surviving against the elements and enemies was a challenge.

Early longhouses had the appearance of long, narrow buildings with semicircular roofs, that is, roofs shaped like a barrel cut in half lengthwise. Their frames were made from two long rows of saplings placed 10 feet apart. The tops of the saplings were bent over toward the other row and covered with skins or elm bark. Longhouses evolved with higher walls and a more rectangular shape. Eventually, peaked roofs replaced the semi-circular roofs.

Most villages overlooked rivers and lakes and were located on hills for reasons of defense and drainage. The Iroquois built villages with palisades constructed of vertical posts for protection against attack. Gardens were usually located on lower ground below the village. The women and children cultivated corn, beans, and squash in the village garden. Well-tended orchards grew within a short distance of the longhouses.

The Iroquois moved their villages every 10 to 12 years. By that time, they had to travel farther for firewood, and the soil, without fertilization or crop rotation, had become less fertile. It was time to move on. Men chose the new site, cleared it of brush and trees, built new longhouses, and tilled the soil to prepare the garden for planting. Then, if they lived on a river, the family possessions were carried upstream in bark canoes.

Many people, members of multiple families, lived in one longhouse. A village was divided into clans, such as the bear, beaver, deer, eel, hawk, snipe, turtle, and wolf clans. Members of the Bear Clan of a Mohawk tribe were relatives of Bear Clan members of an Oneida tribe. Clan members did not intermarry.

Rows of bunk beds lined the inside walls of the longhouse. Each family unit had a 12-foot section of the dwelling with bark interior partitions for privacy. Each family also had a fire pit with an overhead hole in the roof to allow smoke to escape. Longhouses were dark; the only light entered through doorways or smoke holes. Babies were kept on cradle boards or in papooses until they were about two years old; then they toddled around the longhouse.

Change of seasons was important to the Iroquois. They viewed winter as a time to renew the body and the mind. They held midwinter ceremonies in January and February to welcome in the New Year and participated in dances and competitive games. False Face Society members, who wore masks representing healing spirits, danced around the longhouse fire and spread ashes around those who were ill to drive away evil spirits. Members of the Cornhusk Society, who wore masks made from cornhusks, also participated in the midwinter ceremonies to thank the spirits for the harvest.

Snow snake was one of the winter games played by the Iroquois. They crafted snakes from flexible pieces of wood over six-foot long. Two eight-player teams alternated in tossing the snakes across a track of ice from which the snow had been brushed. Points were awarded based on the distance snow snakes traveled over the ice.

In early March, Iroquois women moved the fire outdoors, and men worked outside on warm days making and repairing fishing nets. Early spring was also the time for collecting and boiling maple sap to make maple sugar and syrup.

"Inside an Iroquois Longhouse," Rochester Museum & Science Center Diarama

95

Tree bark was gathered in the springtime to make and repair lodge coverings and canoes. The Iroquois made a cut at the base and another about six feet up the trunk of birch, elm, hickory, and oak trees. After joining the two circular cuts with a vertical cut, they used a wooden wedge to gently peel off bark from the tree. Twine was made from the inner bark of selected trees.

Spring was also the time for planting seeds for the year's crop. Women did the planting, weeding, and harvesting of the major crops of beans, corn, and squash. Each clan cultivated their own plot, as directed by clan mothers. They planted their seeds when the leaf of the oak tree was the size of a mouse's ear. Seeds were blessed, soaked in water for several days, and planted in mounded hills about five feet apart. Women also grew gourds to fashion into bowls, cups, and dippers for water.

During the summer, women and children gathered wild food, such as berries and roots. Men fished, hunted, and worked around the longhouse. In early June, strawberry festivals were held in honor of the first fruit to ripen. The Iroquois considered strawberries sacred, believing that they lined the path to the Great Spirit. The green corn ceremony was held in mid-August to thank the corn spirits for an abundant harvest and to invite them to return during the following growing season. Games such as lacrosse were played during the summer, and ash-splint baskets and clay pots were made during the warm months.

In the autumn, men hunted and trapped, and women harvested and preserved vegetables. Women dried corncobs on wooden boards, which allowed air to circulate around them. Then they scraped kernels off the cobs and stored the corn in bark-lined pits in the ground below the frost line. The corn was thus preserved and protected from scavenging animals. Women also dried beans and squash, which was cut into thin strips and draped from long lines to dry. Also in the fall, women and children gathered beechnuts, butternuts, chestnuts, hazelnuts, hickory nuts, and acorns from which to make flour.

Men used deadfalls, snares, and tomahawks to kill small animals. Deadfalls were heavy logs or stones that fell and crushed the animal when a trip was sprung. Before they received guns from European settlers, they used bows and arrows to kill large animals, such as bear, deer, and elk. Women made breechcloths, dresses, leggings, pants, robes, shirts, and skirts from doeskin; it was lightweight and supple.

"Seneca Village Life," Rochester Museum & Science Center Diarama

The Iroquois knew how to use the products of the wild to their advantage and how to survive harsh northern winters. Until the Revolutionary War, when many of their crops, orchards, and villages were destroyed by General Sullivan's expedition to central New York State, the Iroquois Confederacy was one of the most advanced Indian cultures on the North American continent.

The New Religion of Handsome Lake

In June 1799, three men with red-painted faces and feathered head-dress garbed in traditional Iroquois clothing appeared to Seneca medicine man Handsome Lake while he was in a coma suffering from chronic alcoholism. They bore messages from the Creator that he must:

- Promote temperance within the Iroquois community.
- Encourage witches to repent and to confess their sins.
- Demand that medicine societies be disbanded.
- Ensure that the strawberry festival be reinstated in June when wild strawberries ripen. It was a happy time celebrated with a non-alcoholic strawberry drink. The coming of summer brought a sense of well-being to the community. The strawberry festival began and ended with a thanksgiving speech.
- Spread these messages to the Iroquois nations.

Later, Handsome Lake was visited by a fourth emissary from the Creator, informing him that he should ensure that the traditional ceremonies of the Iroquois continue, particularly the midwinter ceremony that celebrated the transition from the old year to the new. This ceremony marked the passage from a time of darkness to the season of light. Babies born during the last half-year were named during this time. Handsome Lake added four rituals to the traditional midwinter ceremony: the feather dance, the thanksgiving dance, the rite of personal chant, and the bowl game, later called the peach stone game because it was played with peach stones painted a different color on each side.

The new religion founded by Handsome Lake was called "Gai'wiio," or "Good Message." In his New Religion, Handsome Lake de-emphasized the matrilineal society and placed greater emphasis on the family unit, husband and wife, than in the Old Religion. He believed that less emphasis on the matrilineal aspects of the Iroquois would reduce the frequency of mothers recommending that their married daughters divorce their husbands. With the passing of the Society of the Longhouse, he thought that the bond between husband and wife should be stronger than that between mother and daughter.

In the New Religion, great emphasis was placed on raising children. Parents were encouraged to love their children and to keep them in good health. Handsome Lake encouraged the education of children, including education in English-speaking schools. Violent punishment of children, such as striking or whipping, was discouraged.

Older community members were respected, especially on ceremonial issues. Jealousy was discouraged in the New Religion. Jealousy among chiefs and sachems was thought to have caused dissension within the Iroquois community, contributing to the decline of the Confederacy. The New Religion of Handsome Lake made it more acceptable for men to work in the fields and to raise animals for food. Handsome Lake emphasized accommodation with the White society. The religious revivalism of the New Religion revitalized the spirit of the Iroquois Confederacy, while providing a bridge with the past and allowing individuals to retain their identity.

Upon Handsome Lake's death in 1815, the beliefs of his religion were passed on to his grandson, Jimmy Johnson, and to Owen Blacksnake. Blacksnake also taught the New Religion to Henry Stevens, who passed it on to Edward Cornplanter. From the mid-1800s onward, the New Religion of Handsome Lake, also called the Code of Handsome Lake, was followed by one-quarter of all Iroquois.

The Evolution of Lacrosse

Lacrosse originated with the North American Indians, who played the game long before the Europeans discovered America. Nicholas Perrot, an agent of the French Government and a trader, provided one of the earliest descriptions of the game:

> The [Indians] have a certain game of "cross" which is very similar to our tennis. They match tribe against tribe and if their numbers are not equal, they withdraw some of the men from the stronger side. They are all armed with a "cross" stick which has a large portion laced with a racket. The ball with which they play is of wood and nearly the shape of a turkey's

egg. It is the rule of the contest that after a side has won two goals, they change sides of the field with their opponents, and that two out of three or three out of five goals decide the game.

Native Americans played the game from the time that ice melted until harvest time. The game was played by boys, girls, men, and women. Frequently, arms and legs were broken, and a crippling injury was not an infrequent occurrence. Occasionally, participants were killed. Usually, players who were killed had been obstinate and had refused to relinquish the ball. When this happened, the player's body was carried to his lodge in disgrace. Participants did not complain about injuries; they considered them part of the game.

French missionaries among the Hurons called the game "bagga-tie-way" or "le jeu de la crosse." Usually, 400 to 500 players were involved in a game, pitting one village against another, but as many as 2,000 participants engaged in some games. When a famine or a serious epidemic occurred, medicine men called for a game of lacrosse to appease the spirits. Most of the tribe participated, and ceremonies and religious dances were held when the game was over. Some members of the tribe were chosen to impersonate the evil spirits and to be punished. If some of the impersonators died, the spirits were appeased.

Lacrosse was played on all important occasions, particularly when entertaining guests. Rivalry between tribes was fierce. A championship game was an important event, and players fasted for the last day and night before the game. Prayers to the Great Spirit were offered for days leading up to the championship. Native Americans viewed the game as exercise to prepare their bodies for battle. They also considered it training in the tactics of attack and defense.

Author Stephen Powers commented on the game of lacrosse as played by Pomas Indians in California: "They played it with a ball rounded out of an oak knot, propelled by a racket constructed of a long slender stick bent double and bound together leaving a circular hoop at the end, across which is woven a coarse mesh-work of strings. Such an instrument is not strong enough to bat the ball but simply to shove or thrust it along the ground."

Many variations of the game existed. Some tribes played with two goals about 150 feet apart. The Choctaws played with two lacrosse sticks but with only one goal; the goal was made of two poles that were approached from 60 yards away. The distance between the goals was 500 to 600 paces on some playing fields and up to one or one and a half miles on others. Having 80 to 100 players on a side was common. Many southern tribes played with two sticks between which the ball was caught. They were shorter than the single lacrosse sticks used by the northern tribes. The double sticks measured about two feet long. Native Americans on the Pacific Coast started the game by throwing a doeskin ball into the air. The ball was thrown by a maiden chosen for her beauty. Throwing the ball in a way that gave one side the advantage was a serious offense. Even a maiden's beauty would not protect her from punishment if she favored one side with her throw.

Considerable variety also existed in the players' clothing. Biographer Domench described one costume: "The players were costumed with short drawers, or rather a belt, the body being first daubed with a layer of bright colors. From the belt, which is short enough to leave the thigh free, hangs a long animal tail. Round their necks is a necklace of animals' teeth to which is attached a floating mane dyed red, as is the tail, falling as a fringe over chest and shoulders."

Gradually, the game of lacrosse evolved. The large numbers on each side were reduced to 14 or 15. The wooden ball was replaced by one made of scraped deerskin stuffed with deer hair and sewed with sinew. The early single bowed stick and the double sticks strapped together evolved to a single stick with strong netting.

Considerable speculation exists about the first Indian nation to play lacrosse. Many Native-American nations claim to have originated the game, but the most convincing claim is that of the Iroquois Confederacy of New York State.

The Use of Wampum

According to legend, when Deganawida, the peacemaker, approached the land of the Iroquois in an attempt to bring peace to the five nations that were to become the Iroquois Confederacy, he crossed Oneida Lake. He saw many small purple and white shells sticking to his canoe paddles. As he approached the far side of the lake, he noticed piles of shells along the shoreline. He filled deerskin bags with shells and, at his rest stops, strung the shells on deer sinews and then attached the strings together.

On the first wampum belt that he made, he used purple shells for the pictorial figures and white shells for the background. Five symbols representing the original Five Nations were interwoven with five men clasping hands representing brotherly union. He created other belts that represented, for example, some law or council ceremony, death, war, peace, or civil proceedings, such as the installment of a chief. Purple shells were a sign of mourning and war, and white shells symbolized peace.

Wampum belts that were the symbols of law, "Ote-ko-a," were woven of purple and white cylindrical beads about three-sixteenths of an inch long. Purple beads were fashioned from the purple spot in the clam shell, and white beads were made from the conch shell. Most of the older belts were strung on twisted threads from the inner bark of the elm tree, separated by strings of buckskin. The belt was joined together with fine threads of deer sinew.

Wampum beads, strung in lengths of four inches to a foot, were used as a message of peace or war. White beads were used in a "peace string"; a "war string" was made of purple beads. Belts of purple wampum were symbols of death, and if decorated with a red feather or red paint signified war. These belts were used as ransom for a life or for multiple lives.

Councils were convened when a string of wampum was carried by a runner from nation to nation. Actions of a council were neither proposed nor ratified unless sealed by wampum, and a treaty was not considered valid until wampum belts had been exchanged.

One of the finest wampum belts in the possession of the Onondaga Nation is the "George Washington belt," which was exchanged at a peace treaty during Washington's presidency. It has 15 rows of 650 beads each, for a total of 9,750 beads. The symbol of a house with a gable roof and an open door is woven from white beads on a background of purple beads.

Men on both sides of the door, "guardians of the door," are depicted clasping hands with other men, six on one side and seven on the other side of the open door. The clasped hand signifies unity or "the unbroken chain of friendship." The house represents the hall of the United States Government, and the open door connotes peace. The 13 men clasping hands with the "Keepers of the East and West Doors" symbolize the 13 colonies.

Sky Woman's Turtle, Courtesy Iroquois Indian Museum, Howe's Cave

CHAPTER 8

IROQUOIS ORIGIN LEGENDS

"In the numerous Iroquois myths relating to the origin of both ani-
mate and inanimate objects in nature, there appears a reflex of the
Indian's mind as he solves, to his entire satisfaction, mysteries, many
of which are the 'burning questions' of this enlightened age. These
tales vary only with the temperament of the narrator or the exigencies
of the locality. Where oft repeated, they have in time been recorded
in the hearts and minds of the people either as myths or folklore,
embodying the fossilized knowledge and ideas of a previous age."

Erminnie A. Smith, *Myths of the Iroquois*

The Sky-woman and the Turtle

Above the sky was another world where the Great Chief of the Up-above-world and his people, the Celestial Beings, lived. This world was like an enormous cloud that floated in whatever direction the Great Chief wished it to go. A huge tree grew in the center of the Up-above-world. It bore beautiful flowers and healthful fruit that sustained the Celestial Beings. A large, bright blossom grew from the top of the tree and illuminated the world above it. Incense similar to the smoke of sacred tobacco emanated from leaves that grew from the roots of the tree. The roots grew long in the thin crust of earth but not deep.

The lodge of the Great Chief was near the tree, which was the hub of the people's daily activities. The Great Chief had a dream that he was to take a particular fair maiden as his wife. He embraced her and found that she pleased him. He took her to his lodge, and they ate the marriage bread. However, he did not trust her. The Great Chief fell into a restless sleep and had a dream about uprooting the celestial tree to relieve his troubled spirit and to spite his wife. The next morning, he told his wife about the dream and of his intention to uproot the tree at the center of his people's life. She dreaded what life in the Sky World would be like without the tree that sustained them.

The Great Chief gathered his people around the tree and told them to uproot it. They tried with all of their strength, but the roots were too long; they could not pull the tree out of the earth's crust. The Great Chief grew angry with the people for their weakness. He wrapped his strong arms around the trunk of the tree and, with a mighty effort, uprooted it and threw it a great distance. Fruit, leaves, and seeds were shaken from the tree's limbs and were scattered all around the huge hole where the tree had been.

The Great Chief returned to his lodge and told his wife that he had enacted his dream. She expressed her interest in looking into the hole. The Ancient One led her to the spot where the tree had been and told her to sit on the rim of the gaping hole. The Great Chief's anger returned as he looked at her sitting by the edge. He did not feel relieved by the action he had taken, and his wife did not seem to care one way or another. In his aggravated state, he pushed her into the hole. As she slipped downward, she grabbed at the earth on the rim, and gathered many of the fallen seeds and leaves into her hands, along with a piece of the tree's root.

Since the hole went completely through the thin crust of the Celestial World, she found herself in a free-fall. Creatures gathered around the waters below. They could see Sky-woman falling toward them and knew that there was no place for her to live. Four creatures, the Spirits of the Defending Face, the Heavy Night, the Thunder, and the Wind, considered how to provide for her. They sent duck-creatures up into the sky to meet her and to break her fall. The ducks interlocked their wings and guided her gently to the surface of the water below. The great turtle came up from the Under-world to provide a resting place for Sky-woman. His shell became an island.

However, they needed some earth to place on the back of the turtle to make the island inhabitable. A duck dove to the bottom of the water to bring up some earth, but the water was too deep; the duck inhaled water and died. The next attempt was made by a pickerel, but the fish died of its exertions. Finally, a muskrat was successful in reaching the bottom and bringing up a small quantity of earth on its nose. The muskrat spread the earth around on the shell of the turtle. The amount of earth and the size of the turtle grew.

Sky-woman rose up from the prone position in which the ducks had placed her on the turtle's back. As she sat up, she placed the seeds and leaves that she had grasped as she fell from the Up-above-world into the folds of her dress. She took the earth from the Celestial World in her hands, spread it around, and dropped the seeds into it, causing them to germinate. She planted the root that she had grabbed as she was falling. It grew into a tree bearing flowers and fruit; a blossom grew at the top of the tree that illuminated Sky-woman's new world.

The Good Brother and the Bad Brother

Sky-woman was expecting a child when she came down to earth from the Up-above-world, the Celestial World above the sky. She gave birth to a daughter, who was a great comfort to her as the child matured into a young woman. Her daughter roamed about the island on which they lived and told her mother what she saw.

One day, the daughter laughed as she swung from a vine. Sky-woman told her that she sounded as if she was being embraced by a lover and asked her if she had seen a man. She replied that she had not, but that when she swung on the vine she sensed someone nearby; she felt as if her body was being embraced by strong arms, and it caused her to tingle and laugh. Skywoman sensed what had happened, and told her daughter that she was married to Ga-ha. Her mother said that Ga-ha would be the father of her children, and that she would have two sons.

As foretold, Sky-woman's daughter gave birth to two sons: the Good-minded and the Bad-minded. The Good-minded was born first, but she died giving birth to the Bad-minded. Sky-woman buried her daughter in a shallow grave. In time, a tobacco plant grew from the soil above her head, corn grew from the site of her breasts, squash from the location of her abdomen, beans from the area of her fingers, and potatoes from the soil above her toes.

The Good-minded had a gentle nature and grew up with a desire to create. He created the sun, the moon, and the stars to regulate the days, months, seasons, and years. He also created trees for the forests, animals to inhabit the forests, and fish to swim in the lakes and streams.

As soon as the Good-minded had created something good and useful, the Bad-minded followed it with something evil or harmful. The Bad-minded created snakes and lizards and added many small bones to fish to make them difficult to eat. He also placed many rocks, waterfalls, and whirlpools in streams so that they would not be easily navigable. The Bad-minded created many briars, thornbushes, and poisonous plants to make it difficult to walk through the forests.

Eventually, the Good-minded realized that he was going to have to fight his brother and either destroy him or banish him. The Bad-minded challenged his brother to fight, with the agreement that the winner of the fight would govern their universe. First, the Bad-minded tried whipping his brother with reeds; then he tried stabbing him with deer antlers. The fight went on for two days in a howling wind. Many trees were uprooted. Finally, the Good-minded subdued his brother and crushed him into the earth. As he was dying, the Bad-minded told his brother that, after his death, they would have equal power over mankind's souls. The Bad-minded sunk into the eternal pit and became the Evil Spirit.

The Good-minded continued to create and became known as the Great Spirit. He created man and woman and told them to multiply.

The Hand of the Great Spirit
According to legend, the Finger Lakes were made by the impression of the hand of the Great Spirit on central New York State. However,

there are six major Finger Lakes; west to east they are Canandaigua, Keuka, Seneca, Cayuga, Owasco, and Skaneateles.

As told in Iroquois legend, the Great God Manitou wanted to reward the Iroquois Confederacy for its courage in battle and its devotion to the Great Spirit. He decided to bring a part of their happy hunting ground down from the heavens.

The legend tells us that there are six Finger Lakes because the hand of Manitou slipped when he was pushing the portion of Indian paradise down from the heavens, causing six indentations in the earth—and later six lakes—instead of five.

Birth of the Seneca Nation

The foremost legend of Canandaigua Lake is the one that describes the birth of the Seneca Nation. The Senecas believed that many years ago, the forefathers of their nation appeared out of the side of a majestic hill after the Creator opened the earth. The east side of the hill is called South Hill, the south side is called Sunnyside, and the west side is called Whaleback. It is located south of Bare Hill on the east side of the lake several miles north of Woodville, which is across the lake.

The Senecas viewed South Hill with awe, since they considered it the birthplace of the Seneca Nation. They believed that the earth opened, and the first Senecas arrived in the world in an ancient cave in a gorge, called Clark's Gully today, adjacent to West River. This deep gorge, on the east side of the hill, rises 1,100 feet above the valley floor.

The Origin of All Legends

Many years ago when a young Iroquois orphan boy grew to be tall and strong, his foster mother gave him a bow and arrow and told him that it was his responsibility to keep the family provided with birds and small game. One afternoon, as he rested on a large rock, he heard a voice ask him if he would like to hear stories of the Iroquois who had lived before him.

The young boy looked around, but he could not see anybody. Then he realized that the voice was coming from the rock upon which he was sitting. The voice asked him to leave, as an offering, the birds that he had killed earlier that day. The voice told stories of adventures and battles and tales of flying heads and stone giants. The boy was fascinated. The voice stopped at sundown, and the young orphan left his birds at the rock and started home to his lodge.

He shot more birds on the way home, but he had so few when he arrived there that his foster mother scolded him. The next day, he went to the rock again and again left the birds that he had killed as an offering. He told some of his friends about the voice coming from the rock, and they went with him. They also left small game as an offering at the rock and were captivated by the stories told by the mysterious voice.

On the following day, two men followed the boys to see why they had brought home so little game from their hunting trips. As soon as the voice began to speak from the rock, the men came out from their hiding place and listened with the boys. That evening, they told the chief about the stories, and, the next day, the entire tribe came to hear them. They brought offerings of cornbread and venison and listened attentively to the stories emanating from the rock. At the end of the day, the voice invited them to come back the following day.

When they returned the next morning, the Voice of the Rock continued with stories for what was to be the last time. At sunset, the voice told them to remember the stories well, because he would not return. The voice encouraged them to pass the stories on from generation to generation; he would not be telling them again. That was the source of the Iroquois legends. The Confederacy's storytellers have been telling them ever since.

The Origin of Rorick's Glen

Chiwenah, a beautiful Iroquois maiden, was deeply in love with a young brave, Mintowan, of her tribe. They had grown up together, and she loved him for his compassionate nature, his strength, and his reputation for good judgment. However, Mintowan was in love with a young maiden from a neighboring tribe. When Mintowan married his loved one, Chiwenah was crushed. She sat in the doorway of her father's lodge and wept disconsolately.

She wept so hard and for so long that her tears formed a furrow down the nearby hillside. Eventually, a spring pushed through the surface of the ground, and its waters joined with Chiwenah's tears. The furrow in the hillside grew deeper and deeper until it became the gorge that Elmirans know as Rorick's Glen.

Nancy Jemison's Cabin, Letchworth State Park

CHAPTER 9

SELECTED IROQUOIS LEGENDS

"The principal monuments of the once powerful Iroquois are their myths and folklore, with the language in which they are embodied. As these monuments are fast crumbling away, through their contact with European civilization, the ethnologist must hasten his search among them in order to trace the history of their laws of mind and the records of their customs, ideas, laws, and beliefs. Most of these have been long forgotten by the people, who continue to repeat traditions as they have been handed down through their fathers and fathers' fathers, from generation to generation, for many centuries."

Erminnie A. Smith, *Myths of the Iroquois*

109

The Legend of the Star Maidens

Many years ago, a young Iroquois man was walking along a river in what is now central New York State when he found a clearing marked with a circular path formed by the tread of many moccasined feet. He recognized immediately that it was a ring made by Star Maidens when they came down to earth from Sky Land. That night when the moon, called the Sister of the Sun by Native Americans, was high in the heavens, the young man hid in the tall grass near the clearing. He could hear soft music playing in the distance.

He looked up and saw a small white cloud in the sky that appeared to be moving toward the earth. When it came closer, he saw that it was a willow basket containing 12 beautiful maidens. The basket landed softly in the tall grass nearby, and the maidens stepped out of their conveyance into the magic circle in the clearing. They danced with such grace and precision that the onlooker was captivated.

His gaze focused on the youngest of the 12, who appeared to be the most beautiful. The young man, who had decided to ask the delicate young maiden to be his bride, rushed from the tall grass toward her. However, she quickly ran from him toward the willow basket. Before he could stop them, the young women had climbed into the basket and were wafted upward toward Sky Land.

The young man came back again the next night and, using some of his tribal magic, turned himself into a tree. The Star Maidens returned, and, as they danced, the youngest walked near the tree. He turned back into his human form and, taking the maiden into his arms, carried her back to his lodge. He was very tender with her, and soon she returned his love and accepted his marriage proposal. Although her marriage was blessed by the birth of a son, she missed her sisters, parents, and friends. One day, she wove a basket out of willow and, taking her young son with her, returned to Sky Land.

Her husband was overcome with grief. He returned to the circle in the clearing, hoping to see his wife again. Eventually, when their son had grown into a young man, she returned with him to Earth Land. Her husband was overjoyed. He was so happy to be reunited that he agreed to return with them to Sky Land. Before they went up to the heavens, she told him to bring a feather from every bird and a claw or bone from every animal that he had killed in the hunt.

He took this collection with him when he was transported skyward with his wife and son. Upon their arrival in Sky Land, the husband distributed the bones, claws, and feathers. Everyone who received a bone or claw turned into that animal. Those to whom he gave a feather were changed into a bird. The husband, wife, and son each took a feather from the white wood dove. They were all changed into that beautiful bird and flew down to earth, where their descendants can be seen today.

The Sun, the Moon, and the Morning Star

The Iroquois considered the Sun, the Moon, and the Morning Star gods that exerted influence and power over human destiny. They thought that the Sun was created by the Earth Mother who had given birth to the twins, the Bad-minded and the Good-minded, who in turn, created humans, animals, birds, fish, trees, and all other living things. Native Americans considered the Sun a god of war and the messenger of the Sky Chief. The Sun rested in the Celestial Tree in Sky Land, rose in the eastern sky, and watched over the daily activities of the people below. In the evening, the Sun returned to his place of repose in Sky Land and told Sky Chief all that he had observed on earth that day.

The Moon was known as Grandmother / Grandfather, the most mysterious of all bodies in the heavens. She was followed by men for signs of good luck with the hunt. She was also worshiped by women, who prayed to her for the good health of the tribe.

The Morning Star was also thought to be one of the principal beings in the sky and could be viewed as either feminine or masculine. Her appearance in the morning sky was recognized as an omen, either for good or for evil. As a good omen, she was seen as the rescuer of starving families during famine. As an evil omen, she was envisioned as an enchantress who lured hunters from their path and then left them to wander around lost.

The Sun, the Moon, and the Morning Star were but three of the many influences on the Iroquois. Other influences included the Frost God, the Spirit of Spring, the Storm Wind, and the Winter Spirit.

The Maid Who Fell in Love with the Morning Star

One night a beautiful Iroquois maiden slept outside the door of her lodge on sleeping robes that she had spread in the tall grass. While she slept, a shaft of light from above fell upon her face and seemed to touch her gently. When she awoke, she realized that the light had come from the Morning Star up above in Sky Land.

The caress of the tender glow moved her so deeply that she fell in love with the source of the silvery radiance from the heavens. She pledged that she would never marry a mere mortal; she would marry the Morning Star or not marry at all. She stared upward toward Sky Land every night until the brightness of the sun caused the light of her jewel in the heavens to fade. She watched her celestial lover at night and thought about him every day.

One morning she went to a spring near her lodge and was surprised to encounter a handsome young man whom she did not know. He smiled and told her that he was the Morning Star. He said that he knew that she had been looking at him, and that he also knew what was in her heart. He asked her to marry him, and she accepted his proposal. Morning Star removed a long, yellow plume from his hair and handed it to her. As soon as she grasped it in her hand, she was lifted into Sky Land where she was welcomed into Morning Star's lodge.

She lived in her husband's lodge in comfort and was free to go anywhere that she chose. Her only restriction was that she was not to go near a strange golden plant that grew outside of their lodge. One day she could not contain her curiosity any longer, and she pulled the plant out of the ground to see what was beneath it. She found that the hole through which she had entered Sky Land was underneath the curious plant. When she looked through the hole, she could see the people of her village on earth below. She could hear the voices of her friends. She became very homesick and began to cry.

Morning Star found her weeping and knew immediately what she had done. He commanded her to return to her people. She returned to earth on strands of silvery web like a strong spider web. Her exile from Sky Land saddened her, and every evening she walked up a nearby hill, lifted her arms skyward, and begged to be united with her husband.

One evening, Morning Star replied to her prayers. He told her that she could never be forgiven; she would never allowed to return to Sky Land. She was deeply saddened to hear this, and the next day she could not be found. Villagers searched the top of the hill, but she had disappeared. They found a tree growing on the spot where she had lifted her arms skyward in prayer. They were not familiar with the strange tree whose branches seemed to droop downward in sadness. We know the tree as the weeping willow.

The Legend of Lelawala

Many years ago, a peaceful Iroquois tribe lived by a great waterfall in what is now western New York State. They called the waterfall "Thunderer of the Waters" and thought that its roar was the voice of the Great Spirit. The tribe had a custom of offering their fairest maiden to the Great Spirit as a sacrifice every year. Chosen at a formal ceremony, she was honored to represent the tribe and thanked the Great Spirit for being selected.

Lelawala, the daughter of Chief Eagle Eye, was the last maiden to be sacrificed. On the day that she was to be offered up, she appeared on the river bank upstream from the Thunderer of the Waters. She was dressed in white doeskin and wore a garland of wild flowers on her head. The older women of the tribe accompanied her.

Lelawala stepped willingly into her white birchbark canoe that had been filled with woodland flowers, waved goodbye to her family and friends, and paddled out into the swiftly flowing river. Many young men looked at her wistfully. Her canoe was propelled by the rapids to the edge of the waterfall, and she was hurled over the brink to her death.

Chief Eagle Eye watched from the riverbank with the rest of the tribe. He did not cry out, because he knew that his daughter had followed the traditions of her people. However, he felt a great anguish, and his heart was broken. Before anyone could stop him, he jumped into his canoe and paddled out into the river. The rapids carried him swiftly over the waterfall, where he joined his daughter in death. According to legend, Lelawala and her father live in a cave behind the waterfall. The tribe discontinued their annual sacrifice; they were a peaceful people, and the loss of Lelawala and her father was too great for them to bear.

The Legend of Mona-sha-sha

An Iroquois hunter, Joninedah, moved away from his village to a temporary location to see if he could improve his luck hunting in a new area. His wife, Mona-sha-sha, and their young child liked their home in a serene glen next to a waterfall. However, Joninedah's luck did not improve, and day after day he came home empty-handed. Mona-sha-sha fished and picked berries while her husband was away hunting during the day.

Every day, Joninedah came home feeling that the evil eye was upon him. Mona-sha-sha tried to console him, but he did not respond to her smiles. In his despair, he was not kind to her, and Mona-sha-sha felt that he no longer loved her. She waited until he was asleep one night, strapped her child in a papoose on her back, and went out into the dark night. High above the waterfall, she climbed into her canoe, paddled downstream, and was dashed over the falls.

In the morning, Joninedah was surprised to find that she was gone. He went to the edge of the stream and noticed that her canoe was not on the shore. When he found his wife and child in the pool at the bottom of the falls, an albino doe and fawn ran by. The Great Spirit used this symbolism to speak of the dead. Overcome with grief, Joninedah plunged his knife into his chest and joined Mona-sha-sha and their child in death.

The Girl Who Was Not Satisfied with Simple Things

An Iroquois maiden, who was not satisfied with simple things, rejected every suitor who showed an interest in her. One was overweight, another did not pay enough attention to his clothing, and a third one spoke too coarsely. Her mother thought that she would never marry; no man would be good enough.

One evening at dusk, a handsome young man arrived at the door of their lodge. The mother invited the young warrior to enter, but he stood in the doorway and pointed at the maiden. He said, "I have come to take you as my wife." His face was radiant by the light of the fire, and he wore a wide belt of yellow and black wampum. He wore two long feathers in his headband and was graceful when he moved.

The mother asked her daughter if she would marry a stranger whose clan she did not know after rejecting all suitors from her own village. The maiden made up her mind without hesitation to marry the handsome young man. She wrapped all of her possessions into a bundle and followed him into the night. As she walked through the darkness, she began to be afraid. She had left the security of her mother's lodge to follow a man about whom she knew nothing.

Her husband-to-be took her by the arm, told her not to be nervous, and said that they were almost at the home of his people. She asked how that could be since they were very close to the river. He told her to follow him down the hill, and they would be home. They walked down a steep embankment to a lodge with a pair of elk horns mounted over the doorway. He told her that she would meet his people in the morning.

The maiden heard strange noises outside of the lodge and was afraid all night. The lodge smelled of fish. She wrapped her sleeping robe tightly around her and waited anxiously for morning to come. In the morning, there was very little sunshine; the sky was hazy and overcast. Her intended gave her a new dress covered with beautiful wampum and told her that she must wear the dress to make herself ready to meet his people.

She told him that she would not wear the dress because it smelled like fish. The young warrior looked angry, but he did not force her to wear it. He told her that he must go away for awhile, and that she was not to leave the lodge or to be afraid of anything that she saw.

The maiden began to question her rash act of coming with this young man who was a stranger to her. She missed the warmth of her mother's hearth. The young woman remembered the good, honest men from her tribe who had asked for her hand in marriage. She realized that if she had been satisfied with simple things, her current predicament would not have happened.

As she reminisced, a large horned serpent crawled in through the door. He slithered up close to her and stared into her eyes. His body was encircled by bands of yellow and black. She was terrified. Finally, he turned around and went back out through the door. She followed him to the doorway. She looked out and saw serpents everywhere. Some were crawling out of caves, and others were lying on the rocks. Suddenly, the maiden realized that her betrothed was not what he appeared to be. He was a serpent masquerading in human form.

The maiden may have been foolish, but she had courage. She began to consider ways to escape. She decided that she would never put on the dress that he had asked her to wear, for that would probably turn her into a serpent. She continued to think about means of escaping; however, she was very tired because she had gone all night without sleep. Finally, she could no longer hold her eyes open, and she fell asleep.

Her grandfather appeared to her in a dream and offered to help her out of her predicament. He told her to leave the lodge immediately and to run to the steep cliff at the edge of the village. He encouraged her not to turn back, because the serpents would stop her.

When the young woman awoke, she looked out and saw her

betrothed, dressed again as a handsome man, returning to the lodge. She realized that she had to move fast, or she would be trapped there forever. She dashed out of the door and headed for the cliff. The young man called for her to return; but she ran as fast as she could for the high ground, which seemed far away. She could hear rustling noises behind her and the voice of the young warrior calling to her to turn back.

She climbed as a driven person, using all of her strength. Her hands were scraped and bleeding, and she was very tired. When she reached the top of the cliff, she felt her grandfather reach out to help her. Then she looked back and saw many horned serpents along the shoreline and in the river below. Her grandfather, Heno the Thunderer, began to hurl bolts of lightning down on the serpents. Peals of thunder accompanied the flashes of lightning that struck and killed every one of the monsters.

The Thunderer looked down on her, and a gentle rain began to fall. She had been brave, he said, and she had helped him to destroy the great serpents. He told her that her deed had empowered her, and that he might call upon her again for help. Then Heno raised his hand and beckoned a small cloud to come to him. He helped her onto the cloud, which carried her back to her village.

Shortly after she returned, she married a strong, good-hearted man, and they had many children. Her grandfather visited her often, and she traveled with him to help rid the earth of evil beings. When she grew old, she advised her grandchildren: "Be satisfied with simple things."

The Great Serpent and the Young Wife

A young Iroquois man married a beautiful maiden and was very much in love with her. His three sisters were jealous of their sister-in-law because of her beauty and accomplishments and their brother's love for her. The mean-spirited sisters conceived of a plan to destroy the object of their jealousy.

It was blueberry season, and the sisters invited their brother's wife to join them in picking berries for the family. The young wife collected her baskets and climbed into a canoe to paddle across a large lake to the island where rich blueberry fields were found. She had asked her sisters-in-law if she should prepare a lunch to take with them. They had told her that it was not necessary because the blueberries were so abundant that they would not be there for very long.

The young women beached their canoe on the shore. The young wife wanted to pick berries in the fields near the canoe so that they would have to carry the berries only a short distance. The three sisters wanted to pick farther inland. They complained when their sister-in-law would not come with them, but this was exactly what they wanted. They intended to leave her on the island.

The young wife worked steadily and soon had her large basket filled with the purple fruit. She slung the heavy load onto her back and fastened the burden strap—the gusha'a—around her forehead and walked back to the lakeshore. The canoe was not where they had left it, and there was no sign of her sisters-in-law. Suddenly, she knew what they had done. She should have been more suspicious of their uncharacteristic friendliness. She sat down and cried until she was exhausted.

The young wife felt very alone and was afraid of being attacked by wild animals on the island. For all she knew, the island might contain evil creatures that could change her into a bird or an animal. She was tormented by these thoughts until dusk, when she put her head down and slept. A whooping sound over the lake awakened her. She looked out and saw flickering lights and heard the sound of many voices. The lights moved quickly from the water to the land and formed a circle on the shore.

The young woman hid behind a large log. She saw creatures, which had some of the features of men but who also seemed like animals, meeting in council on the beach. She realized that one of the strange beings was discussing the abandonment of the young woman on the island by her sisters-in-law. They were debating how they could help her. One member of the council pointed out that she must be removed from the island because the berries were poisoned, and, if she stayed, the singing wizard, the "segowenota," would bewitch her.

They asked for a volunteer to carry her across the lake to the land from which she had come. A tall creature with a deep voice offered to do it. The council leader told him that his pride exceeded his courage, and that he would not be allowed to help her. A large hulk of a creature volunteered next and was told that his appearance was too terrifying, and that he would frighten the young wife. Several more beings offered their services and were told that they were not suitable.

117

Finally, a tall, slender creature stood up and said in a decisive voice that he would do everything within his power to help the young woman. The council chief responded immediately, "You are the chosen one. You are close to the people!" The council adjourned and the flickering lights reappeared over the lake. The young wife crawled back to the place where she had slept the previous evening. She was very apprehensive as she put her head down and tried to sleep.

Just before dawn, the young woman heard a voice calling to her from the lake. She ran to the shore and saw what appeared to be a huge canoe in the water. She looked closely and saw that it was a large serpent with curved horns on his proud head. He told her that he had come to rescue her, and that she should sit upon his head and hold onto his horns. He told her first to break 12 rods from a willow tree to use as whips if he slowed down on their journey.

The young wife climbed upon the serpent's head and placed the 12 willow whips in her lap. The serpent began to move through the water in a smooth, undulating motion. The girl was far enough above the surface of the water to stay dry. He told her that he was a member of a race of underwater people who were hated by Heno, the Thunder Spirit. The serpent told her that if Heno's scouts, the small black clouds, spotted them, he would send thunder clouds after them.

The serpent had just told her this when they saw a small black cloud moving toward them and felt the wind begin to blow. The serpent told his passenger to whip him so that they might stay ahead of Heno's warriors. She whipped him hard until most of her willow rods were broken. Dark clouds scudded across the sky, and they heard loud peals of thunder in the distance. The serpent was moving through the water so fast that he was creating foam. The claps of thunder grew louder as the Thunder Spirit came closer.

Heno threw a bolt of lightning that struck a floating oak log near them. The sound of thunder was earsplitting. Many bolts of lightning, which looked like sheets of fire, lit up the lake and the shoreline in the distance. The serpent knew that the race would be close, so he appealed to the young wife to whip him hard with her remaining willow rods. He knew that his strength was failing, but he planned to do everything that he could to get her to the shore. He asked her to burn tobacco in his memory on the lakeshore twice a year if he got her there safely.

A bolt of lightning struck the water next to them, and the serpent told her to jump off because he was going to dive. The young wife was sad that they had come so close to safety but had failed. The serpent plunged below the surface of the lake and disappeared. The black clouds began to disburse, the storm diminished, and the sun broke through the few remaining clouds. As she swam, her high regard for her rescuer left her when she considered that he had abandoned her just before victory was theirs.

She was too tired to swim any longer, and she began to sink. She was surprised to find sand beneath her feet. She waded out of the lake and rested, exhausted and frightened, at the base of a tree. The storm moved on from the area, grumbling that it had failed to kill the serpent, "Djodikwado." After resting, she stood up and looked around, filled with gratitude for her deliverer.

She saw a man with a drooping head, who appeared to be wandering aimlessly in a melancholy state. He had been soaked by the rain and looked by his entire demeanor to be very dispirited. She called out to him, "Husband, oh husband, is it truly you?" He turned to her and exclaimed, "Wife, oh wife, returned living, is it you?"

As they walked, arm in arm, to the lodge, the wife explained to her husband what his sisters had done. The three sisters were surprised to see their sister-in-law. The husband banished his sisters from their home forever. The couple lived a long and happy life in which envy and jealousy had no place.

The Boy Who Lived with the Bears

Hono', a young Iroquois boy, was an unloved and unwanted stepson. His stepfather yelled at him frequently, never complimented him for anything that he did, and complained that he ate too much. Hono' promised to hunt for food for the family when he was old enough to repay his stepfather. He asked his stepfather if he would like him then. His mean stepparent merely growled at him.

The stepfather plotted to rid himself of his stepson. He devised a plan to pretend that he was friendly with the child. He suggested to Hono' that it was time that he began to learn how to hunt and invited him on a hunting trip. The young boy was delighted to be asked, and he accepted without hesitation.

They traveled for a considerable distance through the thicket. Hono' asked his stepfather why they were going though the bushes instead of into the woods where the tribe's hunters went. His stepfather told him not to worry; he was a good hunter and knew of a good place to go. Hono' asked why he did not have a bow and quiver of arrows with which to hunt. He was told that they would come later.

After walking for several miles, his stepfather stopped, feigned surprise, and said, "Look. There is a hole. Hurry, Hono', crawl in there and catch the game. You can be a big hunter now!" Hono' was happy that he could do something to please his stepparent, so he crawled in willingly. He moved on his hands and knees down the long tunnel until he could no longer see clearly. He began to return to where the daylight was still shining in and was surprised to see the opening of the tunnel grow dark. When he arrived at the opening he was astonished to find that a large rock had been rolled in place to close the entrance to the tunnel.

Outside, the perpetrator of this ruse was laughing to himself at how easy the deception had been and was thinking, "Hono' will never be able to push aside that large boulder." The young boy was amazed by what his stepfather had done. He knew that his stepfather disliked him, but he did not think that he would go to this extreme to get rid of him.

Hono' heard voices coming from outside the entrance to the cavern. He could hear a meeting in which his name was mentioned frequently. Someone pulled the boulder away from the opening and called for him to come out of the tunnel. He emerged into the daylight outside of the cave and saw a large gathering of animals sitting in a circle. A porcupine was asking, "Now that the boy has been saved, who will care for him?" All of the animals began to speak at once, and all of them offered to care for him. The porcupine said, "Hold! Everyone cannot take care of him. Let each of us tell the boy of our living habits, our temperament, and the food that we eat, and let him chose which of us will be his guardian."

The animals all described why it would be to the boy's advantage to live with them. Finally, the bear said, "I am old and rather surly, but I have a warm heart. I live happily in summer and sleep much in winter. I eat honey, nuts, and berries." As soon as the bear had stopped talking, Hono' exclaimed, "I would like to live with the bear family." The boy was astounded at the gathering of the animals. They acted as though they were humans instead of animals, and they all talked the same language. He knew that some of them were one another's enemies, but they behaved well during the discussion.

The bear led Hono' to her family's den. She told him, "I wished you to become my grandson, because I have lost one and wished you to take his place and drive away my sorrow." They arrived at a hollow stump and mother bear took Hono' by the neck and lowered him into her den. He looked around and saw that their quarters were comfortable. Hono' shared the bear family's meals of honeycombs and dried berries.

His foster grandmother introduced him to her two grandsons. Hono' was happy that he would have playmates in his new home. He found his two foster brothers to be rambunctious, and they pushed him around frequently. However, he pushed them back, and they played well together.

When summer came, Hono' and the two young cubs offered to help in gathering berries to store for the coming winter. Grandmother bear told Hono' of the problems that they always had when they picked berries. Hunters, unfriendly animals, and large birds of prey tried to attack them in the berry patch. She told Hono' that she planned to dress him as a warrior, to paint his face, and to provide him with a bow and a quiver of arrows. She told him that if any of their enemies appeared, he should yell and shoot his arrows at them.

Hono' accompanied the bear family to the berry fields and shot many of his arrows. Most of his targets were birds. The berry season was followed by autumn, the season in which bears gathered nuts for the coming winter. Grandmother bear reminded them that this was a dangerous time for bears, because many hunters were in the woods. Also, many people roamed the fields in the fall gathering fruit and roots.

They did not see any hunters for many days. Finally, they saw one in the distance. Grandmother bear called him a "Do-sko-a-o," or "brush-in-the-mouth hunter." The hunter was chewing a pine twig, which gave off a scent that provided the bears with an advance warning of his presence. The bears hid in a hollow tree, and the hunter walked by without finding them. Another type of hunter was the heavy stepper, who tromped around in the forest warning everyone of his approach. A third type was the "swinging mouth," who warned everyone by humming or singing as he walked through the woods.

When Hono' and the bears were returning to their den, grandmother bear saw a real hunter coming. They called this hunter "four eyes" because he hunted with a dog. She knew that they were in trouble because very little escaped the attention of this hunter or his dog. She recognized him as Hono's stepfather. She told Hono' that if his stepfather chopped down the hollow tree in which they were hiding, she would leave the tree first, followed by the two cubs and Hono'.

Hono's stepfather set a fire at the base of the tree. He kept cutting the coals of the burned bark away so the flames could devour the dry wood behind the coals. When the tree crashed to the ground, grandmother bear ran away first but was stopped by an arrow through the heart; however, her ghost-body ran on. Hono's stepfather also shot the two cubs as they tried to escape. Hono' crawled out of the fallen tree and cried out to his stepfather, "Are you going to shoot me too?"

Hono's stepfather asked the boy what he had done since he had left him and inquired what he was doing hiding in the tree with the bears. His stepfather apologized for being unkind to him and for killing his friends. He told Hono' that if he had called out, he would not have killed the bears. He was afraid of bear ghosts and thought that now he would always have bad luck. Hono' told him not to worry because now he, Hono', could be useful around the lodge and could hunt. Hono' asked him if he would like him now that he could be useful. His stepfather replied, "Truly." The stepfather never hunted again; Hono' did the hunting for them.

The Legend of the Violets

A young Iroquois chief had served his tribe heroically by accomplishing three things. He had slain the great bird of prey that had swept down from the sky and flown away with small children while they were at play. He had traveled alone to the mysterious witches' caves and obtained magic medicine to save his village from a deadly plague without knowing whether he would be allowed to return. Finally, he had led warriors of his tribe to an overwhelming victory over their most powerful enemy, while distinguishing himself by his leadership and valour.

When he had attacked his enemy's village, he had seen the daughter of their chief and was captivated by her. However, he realized that as long as the two tribes were at war, he could not offer the presents of a suitor, such as fur robes or wampum. He hid in the forest near her village just to see her from a distance. He sang her praises aloud so many times that the birds copied his song. The bear and the fox heard him talk in his sleep of the maiden's charms so often that they thought he was speaking of a beautiful flower.

One day the young maiden ventured beyond the boundary of her village, and the young chief took her into his arms and ran away with her through the woods toward his village. A young man of the maiden's village saw her being carried off and sounded an alarm. Men from the village tracked the young chief and the maiden and caught up with them the next morning.

The maiden had fallen in love with her captor and was now a willing captive. To show the pursuing braves that she wanted to marry the young chief, she stood next to him with the braids of her hair entwined around his neck, indicating that, according to custom, the two young people wanted to marry. Their pursuers were incensed by her response and killed the two young lovers where they stood, with the maiden's hair still encircling her intended's neck.

The men left them; when they returned the next morning, the bodies had disappeared. On the spot where they had been struck down, two clusters of violets grew. People of the village had not seen the fragrant flowers before. Birds carried the seeds of the violets to other countries where young people have the courage to love in spite of obstacles.

The Dancing Children

Many years ago, a party of Iroquois traveled through the woods toward a good hunting ground alongside a beautiful lake. Chief Hah-yah-no, "Tracks in the Water," halted his party on the shore of the scenic lake to thank the Great Spirit for their safe arrival at this bountiful site. He said, "Here will we build our lodges for the winter, and may the Great Spirit, who has prospered us on our way, send us plenty of game and health and peace."

In the fall, after the lodges had been built, the children danced to amuse themselves. They did not have much to do, and dancing became a regular form of recreation for them. One day a strange old man came to watch them. He had silver-gray hair and was dressed in white feathers. He told them not to dance; he said that if they continued with this pastime, evil would come to them. He repeated this warning many times, but the children did not pay any attention to him.

The children decided to have a feast to accompany their dancing and asked for food from their parents to bring to their dancing place by the lake. The adults refused, because they thought that the children would waste the food. The children were sad about this; it would have taken only a little food after each dance to make them happy.

One day, they became very light-headed with hunger as they danced, and they could feel themselves being wafted into the air. They did not know what was happening to them; one of them called out to the other seven not to look back. A woman saw them rise into the air and attempted to call them back without success. She ran to the lodges where members of the tribe called out with offers of food of all kinds, but the children would not, or could not, return, despite the sad cries of their parents.

Only one child looked back, and he became a falling star. The other seven continued to rise and became stars, or what the Iroquois called "Oot-kwa-tah." They viewed the seven stars as a band of dancing children. This legend is reminiscent of the Greek myth of the origin of the Pleiades, the seven daughters of Atlas (Maia, Electra, Celaeno, Taygeta, Merope, Alcyone, and Sterope), who were changed into stars.

Statue of Mary Jemison, Letchworth State Park

CHAPTER 10

IROQUOIS PROFILES

"Convinced that they [the Iroquois Confederacy] were born free, they bore themselves with the pride which springs from that consciousness. Sovereigns they were, and the only accountability they acknowledged was to the Great Spirit.... It was virtually an empire that they raised, and this empire, like the empire of Rome, meant peace within its borders. Before the Europeans came, they had been unquestionably for some generations at peace among them. It was an ideal, an idyllic state of aboriginal life. All of which was to be overthrown by the coming of the White man."

J. K. Bloomfield, *The Oneidas*

Joseph Brant

Joseph Brant, "Thayendanega," was born in 1742 in Ohio, where the Iroquois had supplemental hunting and trapping grounds for their nations in New York State. His father was Nickus Brant and his grandfather was Kryn, also known as Joseph Togouiroui and as the "Great Mohawk." Kryn lived in the Mohawk village at Canajoharie; he and his son, Nickus, were known as fierce warriors. Joseph's sister, Molly, who was to become the wife of Sir William Johnson, Superintendent for the Crown of England of All Northern Indians in North America, was born in Ohio in 1737.

The Brant family returned to the Mohawk Valley in 1750 to find many more European settlers than when they had moved to Ohio. In 1755, Brant traveled with a Mohawk war party that accompanied Sir William Johnson to Lake George, where Brant, at the age of 13, engaged in his first skirmish with the French. His second fight was alongside Mohawk guides who led British redcoats and pioneers to the French Fort Frontenac in Canada.

Brant became friends with William of Canajoharie, son of Sir William Johnson and a Mohawk mother. Younger than Brant but stronger and just as fast, William won most of their fights. Sir William sent Brant and his son, William, to the Moor School at Lebanon, Connecticut, where young Indians learned to translate Greek into English and English into their native language. The headmaster, Rev. Eleazar Wheelock, subsequently moved to New Hampshire and founded Dartmouth College. Samuel Kirkland, who later became a Presbyterian minister working among the Oneidas, was a fellow student. Brant taught the Mohawk language to Kirkland, who helped Brant with his English.

In 1759, Brant and William of Canajoharie both left school to fight for the British at Niagara. In 1763, the Seven Years War was ended by the Treaty of Paris, and the Iroquois were no longer able to maneuver the British and the French against each other. Brant accompanied Sir William Johnson to Detroit as an interpreter. He continued to educate himself and acted as an advisor to Johnson on Indian affairs. Brant joined the Church of England and assisted with the translation of the New Testament into the Mohawk language.

In 1774, Sir William Johnson died and was succeeded as Superintendent for Indian Affairs for the Crown of England by his nephew, Colonel Guy Johnson. Brant, whom the new superintendent had appointed his secretary, accompanied Colonel Johnson to Canada the following year where Brant was commissioned captain in the British Army and appointed commander of the Mohawk warriors. At the Battle of St. Johns, Brant and his force of Mohawks helped to delay the brief American foray into Canada.

In 1776, Brant accompanied Colonel Johnson to England where he was presented to King George III, became a Mason, and was well received. George Romney painted his portrait. This visit established Brant's ties with the British. He was interviewed by James Boswell, the biographer of Samuel Johnson, who thought that Brant did not have "the ferocious dignity of a savage leader." Nevertheless, during the Revolutionary War, Brant had the reputation of being a savage warrior. He was blamed for atrocities at the Wyoming Massacre, and he was not even there.

Brant returned to New York later in 1776 and traveled to Canada. In the spring of 1777, Brant reaffirmed his support for the British at a conference with American General Nicholas Herkimer at Oquaga on the Susquehanna River. Brant accompanied British Lieutenant Colonel Barry St. Leger and his force of British regulars, loyal colonists, and Hessian mercenaries to Ft. Stanwix, where they surrounded the 700-man garrison. Molly Brant sent word from Canajoharie that General Herkimer and 800 American militiamen were on their way to relieve Ft. Stanwix.

St. Leger dispatched a force of 70 Whites and 400 Indians, including many Senecas, commanded by Sir John Johnson, son of Sir William Johnson, to intercept Herkimer. Johnson delegated Brant to select a site to ambush Herkimer and his men. The location that Brant selected, five miles from the fort in a marshy ravine near Oriskany Creek, was to become the site of one of the bloodiest battles of the Revolutionary War.

Although Herkimer had Oneida scouts in his party, he did not take the necessary precautions and walked into the trap set by Brant and his Mohawks. Herkimer's troops suffered 500 casualties and failed to relieve Ft. Stanwix. Herkimer was wounded and died after his leg was amputated. The British siege of Ft. Stanwix lasted for another 16 days, but, without sufficient artillery, they were unable to capture the fort.

The Battle of Oriskany further divided the nations of the Iroquois Confederacy. After the battle, pro-British Iroquois destroyed an

Oneida village near Oriskany, and the Oneidas pillaged the Mohawk village of Canajoharie, causing Molly Brant to flee. The Oneidas and Tuscaroras joined Washington's Army, and they supplied the Colonials with food. Many warriors of the other four Iroquois nations fought alongside the British.

From 1778 to 1781, Brant led many raids in the Mohawk Valley and the surrounding region. He opposed General John Sullivan's campaign of destruction through Iroquois country. Brant participated in the Battle of Newtown, where he, Chief Cornplanter, and their force of 1,100 Tories, Canadian Rangers, and Indians were defeated by Generals Sullivan and Clinton. Later, Brant fought alongside Sir John Johnson in the raid on Schoharie. After the British defeat at Klock's Field, Brant escaped to Niagara.

The Iroquois were left out of the peace treaty that ended the Revolutionary War. All of their land was ceded to the United States by Great Britain. The Oneidas and the Tuscaroras initially fared no better than the other four nations of the Confederacy that had sided with the British. However, President Washington and his advisor, Philip Schuyler, advocated a less harsh treatment of the Iroquois nations. Many Iroquois, except for the Mohawks, returned to their home regions.

Brant and the Mohawks preferred to remain in Canada under British jurisdiction. Brant appealed to Ontario Provincial Governor Frederick Haldimand for reimbursement for Mohawk support in the recent conflict. They received financial remuneration and were granted the Six Nations Reservation, which initially was 100 miles long and six miles wide on both sides of the Grand River that flows into Lake Erie. Brant built a church and a school on the reservation. In 1785, Brant visited England a second time and again was well received.

In 1797, the Mohawk Nation ceded all territorial lands in New York State to the American Government. On several occasions, Brant attempted to aggravate the relationship between the Iroquois and the Americans without success. He lived comfortably, supported by the Canadian Government, in a fine house overlooking Lake Ontario near Hamilton. Brant died on November 24, 1807, and was buried near the church that he had built on the Six Nations Reservation, located in the city of Brantford in the township of Brant.

Battle of Newtown Obelisk, Elmira

Handsome Lake

Handsome Lake, "Ganyahdiyoh," was born at Canohwagus (Avon) in 1735. He was a medicine man who became the Turtle Clan League Sachem in 1795. Four years later, he lived with his half-brother, Cornplanter, and suffered from chronic alcoholism. He was cared for by a married daughter who described her father as being nothing but "yellow skin and dried bones." In June 1799, Handsome Lake collapsed and was thought to have died. His nephew, Owen Blacksnake, realized that his uncle had not died but was in a coma. While unconscious, Handsome Lake had a series of visions that changed his life.

Three representatives of the Creator appeared to him and told him to give up drinking or he would die. He was given messages to pass on to the Iroquois to stem the slide of their society and give them back a feeling of self-worth. In time, the New Religion would replace the Old Religion and members of the Iroquois Confederacy would subscribe either to Christianity or to the New Religion.

Handsome Lake regained his health and became an Iroquois prophet spreading the word of his New Religion, "Gai'wiio" (also called the "Good Message"). He visited President Jefferson in Washington to ask for his support. Handsome Lake had subsequent visions and revelations and refined his New Religion over the next 16 years. He accused individuals of witchcraft and denigrated political rivals, such as Red Jacket, causing much dissension.

Handsome Lake opposed land sales by the Iroquois Confederacy and spoke out against Iroquois joining the U.S. military in the War of 1812. After all, Native Americans were not citizens. He advocated eliminating the pagan ceremonies of the Confederacy but retaining many other traditional beliefs. Positive aspects of the New Religion were a renewal of the emphasis on the family and an acknowledgement of the importance of agriculture and the domestication of animals as the reliance on hunting for food decreased.

The New Religion renewed a sense of self-worth among the Iroquois. Author James Wilson wrote about Handsome Lake: "His message allowed [the Iroquois] to adapt, in some measure, to the new society which was rapidly establishing itself around them, and at the same time, to maintain their own identity."

In 1803, Handsome Lake had a disagreement with Cornplanter and moved to the Allegany Reservation, where he established a settlement called Coldspring. At Coldspring, one of his followers, his

Handsome Lake Monument, Onondaga Reservation

nephew, John O'Bail, spoke out against him. In 1809, Handsome Lake moved again—to the Tonawanda Reservation.

Handsome Lake died on August 10, 1815, while visiting the Onondaga Reservation, south of Syracuse. He is buried on the reservation near the Onondaga Council House.

Hiawatha

There were two Hiawathas: the Hiawatha described by Henry Wadsworth Longfellow in *The Song of Hiawatha* and the Onondaga Chief who lived near Syracuse during the 15th century. Longfellow's Hiawatha was based on the legendary Indian hero who, as described by Henry Rowe Schoolcraft in *The Myth of Hiawatha*, could take mile-long steps and turn into a wolf. The Hiawatha described by Longfellow could talk with the animals and outrun an arrow shot through the air. He was an Ojibwa who lived on the shores of Lake Gitche Gumee near Lake Superior, married Minnehaha, met White people, and became a Christian.

The real Hiawatha lived on the south shore of Cross Lake west of Syracuse during the mid-1400s. He was an excellent speaker who became a leader of the Onondaga Nation, married, and had three (seven in some accounts) daughters.

His wife's name is lost to history; it was not Minnehaha. Hiawatha's ideas were different from those of his peers; he spoke of peace, not war. The Iroquois Confederacy, which initially included the Senecas, Cayugas, Onondagas, Oneidas, and Mohawks, was continually at war—sometimes among themselves but usually with other nations, such as the Hurons from Canada and the Susquehannocks south of them.

Hiawatha counseled for friendship among the nations at a time when retribution was important to the Confederacy. If an Iroquois were killed, the victim's male relatives would kill the murderer. If the murderer could not be located, one of his relatives would be killed in his place. Revenge was a way of life; it did not matter if an innocent person lost his life.

An evil character named "Ododarhoh" lived south of the principal Onondaga village. He lived alone in a dark ravine near a marsh and slept on a bed of bullrushes. According to legend, the locks of his long, intertwined hair were living snakes. He was a cannibal who ate men, women, and children raw. The Onondagas feared him as a wizard. Ododarhoh committed the unspeakable crime of killing Hiawatha's wife and three daughters.

Hiawatha threw himself to the ground and thrashed around in anguish. His grief was so deep that people hesitated to approach him and offer their consolation. He left the village, built a lodge of hemlock branches, and became a hermit and an aimless wanderer. Hiawatha was expected to kill Ododarhoh, but it was not his nature to commit an act of revenge that would not bring back his wife and daughters.

When Hiawatha was in the depths of his despair, he was visited at his lodge by Deganawida the Peacemaker. Deganawida was a Huron evangelist who attempted to convince the Iroquois Confederacy to stop fighting among themselves and to live in peace. He did not have much success since he was an outsider and because he stuttered; he was not a good speechmaker. He sought the help of Hiawatha, who was respected within the Confederacy and was an outstanding orator.

Hiawatha immediately became a follower of Deganawida; it was too late for preserving his own family, but perhaps he could work with the Peacemaker to save the lives of others. The ideas preached by Deganawida brought Hiawatha out of his grief. The Peacemaker's scheme to convince the Onondagas and the other nations of the Confederacy to implement plans for peace was to convert Ododarhoh from his evil ways and to use Hiawatha as the instrument of this conversion. If the Onondagas saw that Hiawatha, upon whom Ododarhoh had inflicted such a terrible injustice, could forgive his tormenter and convince him to follow the path of peace, then the rest of the Confederacy would follow.

Deganawida and Hiawatha visited the evil wizard at his lodge in the dark ravine, where Hiawatha placated Ododarhoh by singing to him and speaking the message of peace and of Iroquois unity. Ododarhoh's two visitors expected him to react violently, because they knew of the evil one's opposition to peace and unity. They expected to be attacked, but Ododarhoh said that he would mend his ways and abide by these proposals of peace and unity. Hiawatha then combed the snakes, which symbolically represented evil and insane thoughts, out of the wizard's hair. Thus Hiawatha, "Ayonwartha," was given his name, which meant "He who combs."

The Onondaga Nation followed Ododarhoh into the Iroquois

Confederacy and the Great Peace. An Onondaga village near Syracuse became the capital of the Confederacy and the location of the council fire. Ododarhoh was named "Firekeeper," a position comparable to President of the Senate. He became one of the most powerful of the sachems. Deganawida and Hiawatha traveled from village to village enlisting support for the Confederacy from the five original Iroquois nations.

Hiawatha instituted wampum as money to use instead of revenge. Murderers paid for their crimes in wampum, which was usually made of purple and white shells. Hiawatha was aware that a price could not be set on the value of human life, but it was better for a murderer to pay the victim's family in wampum than continue a progression of retaliatory killings. Wampum was made to carry a message as well as to have intrinsic value.

When Deganawida saw that his objectives had been accomplished, he said, "Now I shall be seen no more, and I go whither none can follow me." Five years after he had arrived among the Onondagas, the peacemaker climbed into a white birchbark canoe on the eastern shore of Onondaga Lake and paddled westward into the sunset. The Iroquois associated white with sacredness. Their canoes usually were made of gray or white bark.

Hiawatha, who watched from the shore, continued the work of Deganawida. Historians know little about Hiawatha's later life. Mohawks claim that he lived among them as an elder statesman who cleared rocks and brush from rivers to make them more navigable and to facilitate communications among the villages.

According to Indian legend, Hiawatha left the Iroquois in the same manner that his mentor, Deganawida, did—paddling a white birchbark canoe westward across a lake. The two men were thought to have found happiness in the Sky World, where strawberries grow as large as apples and flowers of white light always bloom. Hiawatha and the Peacemaker had a lasting influence on the Iroquois Confederacy, which for centuries was the most powerful Native-American Culture in the Western Hemisphere north of Mexico.

Mary Jemison

Mary Jemison, "White woman of the Genesee," was born in 1743 on the sailing vessel, *Mary and William*, en route from Ireland to Philadelphia. Her parents, Thomas and Jane Jemison, settled near

Gettysburg, Pennsylvania. In 1758, during the French and Indian War, the Jemison home was attacked by a party of six Indians and four Frenchmen. They killed and scalped the Jemisons as well as a visiting family. Fifteen-year-old Mary Jemison was spared but was carried off by the Indians.

The Indians traveled west to Fort Duquesne and down the Ohio River by canoe. Mary was placed in the keeping of two Seneca women who had lost a relative in battle. They adopted Mary as a sister, gave her Indian clothing to replace her tattered dress, and named her "Deh-ge-wan-us," which means "Two falling voices." Initially, she missed the society in which she was raised, but she adapted well to Indian life. Mary had many opportunities to leave her Indian captors during her lifetime, but she chose to remain with them. Eventually, her light skin and hair were the only things that distinguished her from other Indian women.

When she was 17, Mary's Indian sisters told her that, according to custom, she must marry. Her sisters' choice for a husband for her was Sheninjee, a Delaware chief. Sheninjee and Mary had a son, who was named Thomas for her father.

Mary's two Seneca sisters returned to their home at the Seneca settlement at Little Beard's Town on the Genesee River. Sheninjee left on an extended hunting trip and told Mary that he would join her at Little Beard's Town. Mary set out on the long eastward journey from Ohio carrying her nine-month-old son, Thomas. She was accompanied by two foster brothers.

Mary's first home in Genesee country was at Caneadea, which was described by the Senecas as the place "where the heavens lean against the earth." At the end of the long trek, Mary rejoined her Seneca sisters at Little Beard's Town, approximately 35 miles north of Caneadea. The following spring, she heard that Sheninjee had been killed. Her second husband was Hiakatoo, a six-foot-tall, 60-year-old Seneca chief. In battle, Hiakatoo was ferocious. He had a reputation for brutality, but he was always kind to his 24-year-old bride. Hiakatoo and Mary had six children, four daughters and two sons.

In 1779, Hiakatoo went off to fight General Sullivan's army. Mary and her children left the village before it was destroyed by Sullivan's men. She moved to the Gardeau Flats, south of Little Beard's Town, and built a cabin. Gardeau, which is now part of Letchworth State Park, was her home for the next 50 years. The

Senecas were kind to Mary; they gave her four acres of land at Gardeau for raising crops.

At the great Council of Big Tree in 1797, the Senecas settled their land claims with Robert Morris, financier of the Revolutionary War. Mary told Thomas Morris, son and agent of Robert Morris, that she had cultivated many areas in the Gardeau Flats; she requested that her tract be expanded. Morris thought that he was giving away about 150 acres, but Mary became the owner of 17,280 acres (27 square miles) of scenic Genesee country known as the Gardeau Tract.

Mary sold her land in the Genesee Valley in 1831 and moved to the Buffalo Creek Reservation. She attended an Indian mission school and converted to Christianity at the age of 89. Mary lived two more years. Her sons all met with violent deaths; her daughters cared for her in her old age. She was buried in the cemetery on the Buffalo Creek Reservation.

On March 7, 1874, William Letchworth had Mary Jemison's remains reinterred on the plateau near Glen Iris Inn in Letchworth State Park with an appropriate ceremony. A monument sculpted by Henry K. Bush-Brown was dedicated at Mary's gravesite on September 10, 1910. The sculpture is of Mary as a young woman with a papoose on her back, as she looked on her trek back from Ohio. A cabin that Mary had built for her daughter, Nancy, was moved to the council grounds near the statue.

Chief Logan

In 1727, Chief Logan, "Tah-gah-jute," a celebrated orator of the Iroquois Confederacy, was born at the Cayuga village of Wasco. Tah-gah-jute was the second son of Shikellimus, a distinguished sachem of the Cayugas, who was appointed Indian agent because he was considered a friend of the White man. Tah-gah-jute received the name of Logan when he was baptized, in honor of James Logan, Secretary of the Province. He embraced not only Christian doctrines but also the pacifism of the Quakers. He and his wife, Alvaretta, were married by a missionary, Reverend David Zeisberger.

Logan ceased being a pacifist when his wife and children were killed by Colonel Cresap, the English leader of a band of ruffians. Logan went on a rampage until 30 scalps hung from his belt. He made one of his more famous speeches just after this incident in a conference with the British Governor of Virginia at the signing of the Treaty of Lord Dunmore, as described in "Jefferson's Notes on Virginia":

> I appeal to any White man to say if he ever entered
> Logan's cabin hungry and he gave him not meat; if
> he ever came in cold and naked, and he clothed him
> not. During the close of the last and long bloody war,
> Logan remained idle in his cabin, an advocate of
> peace. Such was my love for the Whites that my
> countrymen pointed, as they passed, and said,
> "Logan is the friend of the White men." I had even
> thought to have lived with you, but for the injuries of
> one man. Colonel Cresap, the last spring, in cold
> blood and unprovoked, murdered all the relations of
> Logan, not sparing even my wife and children.
>
> There runs not a drop of my blood in any living crea-
> ture. This called on me for revenge. I have sought it.
> I have killed many. I have fully glutted my
> vengeance. For my country, I rejoice at the beams of
> peace. But do not harbor a thought that mine is the
> joy of fear. Logan never felt fear. He will not turn on
> his heel to save his life. Who is there to mourn for
> Logan? Not one.

In 1852, a 56-foot stone obelisk was erected on the site of an ancient altar mound in Fort Hill Cemetery in Auburn in memory of Chief Logan. Inscribed on the obelisk is "WHO IS THERE TO MOURN FOR LOGAN."

Lewis Henry Morgan, "Grand Tekarihogea"

Lewis Henry Morgan was born in 1818 in Aurora, on the eastern shore of Cayuga Lake. After graduating from Union College in Schenectady, he organized the Gordian Knot, a club comprised of graduates of the Cayuga Academy in Aurora. He renamed it the "Grand Order of the Iroquois," which he perceived as a replacement for the fading Iroquois Confederacy.

He founded the Seneca chapter in Waterloo and the Cayuga chapter in Aurora. In 1844, Morgan and his club members initiated Abraham La Fort, an Onondaga, into the Cayuga chapter to learn more about how the Iroquois were organized.

On a trip to Albany, Morgan met Ely Parker, who was in town to interpret for three visiting Iroquois chiefs from the Tonawanda Reservation. Parker introduced him to the chiefs, including Jimmy Johnson, nephew of Red Jacket and grandson of Handsome Lake. Morgan was eager to learn more about the Iroquois chiefs and the organization of the Confederacy. Parker enrolled in the Cayuga Academy but moved to Washington after one year to work with Joseph Henry, the first Secretary of the Smithsonian Institution.

Late in 1844, Morgan moved to Rochester, where he was a successful corporation lawyer and State Legislator. Morgan, who was called "Grand Tekarihogea," established a turtle clan of the Seneca Nation and considered himself a "supreme chieftain of the Iroquois." He invited Henry Rowe Schoolcraft, a well-known geologist, explorer, and ethnologist, to speak at the annual meeting of the Grand Order of the Iroquois in Aurora. Schoolcraft's speech was a plea to Morgan to cease his "adolescent games" and begin a serious study of the Iroquois.

In September 1845, Morgan attended a meeting of the Grand Council of the Six Nations at Tonawanda at which new chiefs were elected. The Senecas, Onondagas, and Mohawks (the older brothers) sat on one side of the hall, and the Cayugas, Oneidas, and Tuscaroras (the younger brothers) sat on the opposite side. Jimmy Johnson spoke for three hours delivering his annual message of Handsome Lake. Morgan was fascinated even though he could not understand a word that was spoken. Parker documented Handsome Lake's teachings at this meeting. This was Morgan's first field trip, which was followed by trips to the Buffalo Creek and Tonawanda Reservations in 1845 and 1846.

Morgan wrote a paper on the Iroquois government and a series of letters for the *American Review*, which were incorporated into his book, *League of the Ho-dé-no-sau-nee, or Iroquois* in 1851. Explorer John Wesley Powell considered this book the first scientific account of Indian Nations acquired by the Bureau of American Ethnology.

In 1847, Governor John Young commissioned Morgan to gather artifacts for the Natural History Museum in Albany. Morgan acquired 478 items on three trips to the Tonawanda and Grand River Reservations in 1849-50. Unfortunately, all but 71 items were destroyed by a fire in the New York State capitol in 1911. In 1848-49, Morgan documented the teachings of Handsome Lake with the assistance of Jimmy Johnson.

In 1851, Morgan married Mary Elizabeth Steele and with her encouragement became a serious student of the Iroquois. Also that year, Francis Parkman published his multiple-volume history of the wars between the French and the British along with an account of their Indian allies. Parkman, who did not consider himself a ethnographer, had visited the Onondaga Nation in 1845. He had difficulty obtaining information from the Iroquois.

Morgan used Parkman's information in addition to that of other authors, including Cadwallader Colden, in his work. Between Parkman and Morgan, the story of the Iroquois began to emerge. By researching the Iroquois, Morgan became a founder of the discipline of anthropology. His contributions were recognized when he joined the American Association for the Advancement of Science in 1856.

Ely Parker

Ely Parker, Seneca chief, lawyer, civil engineer, and Civil War general, was born on the Tonawanda Reservation in western New York in 1828. He was called Ha-sa-no-an-da, "Leading Name," as a child and Do-ne-ho-ga-wa, "Open Door," when he became Grand Sachem of the Iroquois Confederacy in 1851.

Ely's mother, Elizabeth Johnson Parker, was the daughter of Chief Jimmy Johnson (Handsome Lake's grandson) and a grandniece of Red Jacket. Four months before Ely was born, his mother had a dream that foretold her son's life "as a White man as well as an Indian." Because Senecas believed in the symbolism of dreams, she went to a dream interpreter who told her, according to an account by Harriet Maxwell Converse in the January 24, 1897 Buffalo *Express*:

> A son will be born to you who will be distinguished among his nation as a peacemaker; he will become a White man as well as an Indian, with great learning; he will be a warrior for the pale faces; he will be a wise White man, but will never desert his Indian people to "lay down his horns as a great Iroquois chief"; his name will reach from the East to the West—the North to the South, as great among his Indian family and the palefaces. His sun will rise on Indian land and set on the White man's land. Yet the ancient land of his ancestors will fold him in death.

Ely's father, William Parker, a farmer who operated one of the first sawmills on Tonawanda Creek, became a Seneca chief. Ely's oldest brother, Ga-nos-qua, was named Spencer Cone after the Baptist clergyman who educated him. Ely had two other older brothers, Levi and Nicholson; a younger sister, Caroline; and two younger brothers, Newton and Solomon.

Ely attended a Baptist mission school adjacent to the reservation, where he studied arithmetic, grammar, geography, and spelling and developed agricultural skills. Students were encouraged to speak English. The school was run by Reverend Ely Stone, who passed on his first name to young Parker. After graduation, Ely was sent to the Grand River Iroquois Reservation in Ontario, Canada, to increase his knowledge of woodcraft, including archery, canoeing, fishing, and gunnery.

When he returned from Canada, Ely attended Yates Academy in adjacent Orleans County, where he was the only Native-American student. He studied Latin and Greek and mastered English while at the academy and was known for his oratorical ability. Although the school was nonsectarian, its religious emphasis acquainted Ely with Christianity. He was impressed with Christianity, but he was never baptized. Henry Flagler, who was to become an associate of John D. Rockefeller, was a classmate and friend of Ely at the academy.

At the age of 14, Ely became an interpreter for the chiefs of the Tonawanda Reservation. He prepared documents and certified marks and signatures of the chiefs in the written communications that they forwarded to the State and Federal Governments. In 1844, Parker was sent by the chiefs as their interpreter to Albany where he met Lewis Henry Morgan, student of Iroquois culture, in a bookstore. Parker introduced Morgan to his grandfather, Jimmy Johnson, and the other members of the delegation, including Chiefs John Blacksmith and John Bigfire.

The Senecas were in Albany to meet Governor Silas Wright and to protest the sale of the Tonawanda and Buffalo Creek Reservations to the Ogden Land Company in the Compromise Treaty of 1842, in which the Allegany and Cattaraugus Reservations were retained by the Iroquois. Parker wrote a letter of protest to the Secretary of War, whose department at the time included the Office of Indian Affairs. Parker studied at the Yates Academy, while assisting the Tonawanda chiefs, until 1845, when Morgan enrolled Parker in the Cayuga

Academy at Aurora.

Parker's preparation in Greek, Latin, and debating eased his transition to the Cayuga Academy. Morgan formed a club called the "Grand Order of the Iroquois" at Aurora to learn about and preserve Iroquois culture. Parker was made an honorary member to ensure the authenticity of their ceremonies. The Grand Order aided the Tonawanda Senecas in their petition to Washington to preserve their reservation.

Parker visited Washington, D.C., with Chiefs John Blacksmith and Isaac Shanks in an attempt to save the Tonawanda Reservation. They had an audience with President Polk and met with Secretary of War William Marcy and the Commissioner of Indian Affairs. Negotiations dragged on, and the two chiefs returned to the Reservation, leaving Parker to pursue their cause. On one of his trips to Washington, Parker met Henry Clay, who treated him "as an old and familiar friend." On one occasion when Parker was walking in the city, President Polk's wife stopped her carriage to offer him a ride. He was away from school much of 1847.

Parker received an offer to study law with William Angel, District Attorney and Federal Indian Agent in Ellicottville. He began his study by reading Blackstone's *Commentaries*. He was well liked in Ellicottville and was asked to join the Masonic lodge. A precedent had been set by Joseph Brant, the Mohawk Chief, who had been introduced to Masonry in England in 1778.

During the summer of 1848, Angel was removed from his position as Federal Indian Agent for political reasons. Because he lost his mentor and because Indians were not citizens, Parker was never admitted to the bar. He decided to change careers and looked for a position as an engineer. Schools of Civil Engineering did not exist at the time; engineers received their training on the job. His first assignment was on the Genesee Valley Canal between the Genesee River and Hinsdale, near Olean.

From this canal project, Parker moved to the Office of the Resident Engineer for New York State Canals in Rochester. While in Rochester, he helped Lewis Henry Morgan compile information on the culture of the Iroquois Confederacy. In 1851, Morgan published *League of the Ho-dé-no-sau-nee, or Iroquois*, which contained much material obtained from Parker. Morgan dedicated the book to Parker.

In July 1851, Parker returned to the Tonawanda Reservation for a council meeting to elect a new grand sachem to replace John Blacksmith, who had died. The council was attended by the Six Nations of the Iroquois Confederacy. On September 19, 1851, at the age of 23, Parker was proclaimed Grand Sachem of the Six Nations of Indians in New York and Canada. His new name, Do-ne-ho-ga-wa, "Open Door," acknowledged his role as Keeper of the Western Door of the Confederacy.

According to William H. Armstrong in *Warrior in Two Worlds*: Ely S. Parker, Parker was told:

> The thickness of your skin shall be seven spans — which is to say you will be proof against anger, offensive actions, and criticism. Your heart shall be filled with peace and good will and your mind filled with a yearning for the welfare of the people of the Confederacy. With endless patience, you shall carry out your duty and your firmness shall be tempered with tenderness for your people. Neither anger or fury shall find lodgement in your mind and all your words and actions shall be marked with calm deliberation.

During the ceremony, he was presented with the Red Jacket medal, which George Washington had given to Red Jacket in 1792. Parker was told that the medal was a "symbol of the bond of peace which was always to exist between the United States and the Six Nations."

On October 17, 1851, Parker was appointed First Assistant Engineer on State Canals by the New York State Canal Board and became a captain of engineers in the 54th Regiment of the New York Militia. Nevertheless, he continued to represent the Six Nations in their negotiations with New York State and the U.S. Government, which included a trip to Washington in 1856 to meet with President Franklin Pierce.

In his new engineering assignment, Parker transferred his membership in the Masons to Rochester and advanced to the Royal Arch Masons. Although he was the assistant resident engineer, he did the work of the resident engineer, overseeing a staff of 35 men on projects totaling $5 million. He applied for the position of resident engineer, but the position was given to an engineer who had previously held the post. Parker resigned and moved to Norfolk, Virginia, to work on the Chesapeake and Albemarle Ship Canal between Norfolk and the Albemarle Sound in North Carolina.

Parker's next engineering assignment was Superintendent of Construction of a customhouse and a marine hospital in Galena, Illinois. Before beginning his new assignment, he was notified of the decision of the U.S. Supreme Court on the case involving the Tonawanda Reservation. They had ruled that the Ogden Land Company could not remove the Indians from the Tonawanda Reservation as they had been attempting to do. Only the Federal Government could take that action. The Indians' victory protected residents of the reservation from land speculators.

Galena, Illinois, had become an important municipality between Chicago and St. Louis. The region was represented in Congress by Elihu Washburne, who had obtained funds for construction of the two buildings for which Parker was responsible. The buildings were successfully completed, and a staff writer for the Galena newspaper considered the customhouse "the most perfect structure north of St. Louis and south of Chicago." Furthermore, "Mr. Parker has discharged the duties of his important position to the satisfaction of everyone, and by strict attention, impartiality, and perfect knowledge of every branch of of work, contributed, in very great measure, to the successful completion of the building."

Parker met Ulysses S. Grant while living in Galena. As noted by editors James Grant Wilson and Titus Munson Coan in *Personal Recollections of the War of the Rebellion*, Parker described the meeting:

> My acquaintance with the General began in the summer of 1860 at Galena, Illinois, where he was employed in his father's store. I observed at our first meeting how very diffident and reticent he was. It was with difficulty that information on any subject could be obtained from him.... I saw him quite frequently, becoming friendly by degrees as we became better acquainted, which friendship continued to the day of his death.

The Brooklyn *Daily Eagle* quoted Parker in an interview on September 25, 1892. "He [Grant] reminded me of some of my Indian friends. It was necessary to break the ice before the good qualities of the General could be seen." However, Grant could be not only "companionable, but possessed of a warm and sympathetic nature." Parker's participation in the militia and Grant's West Point background provided a common bond. Parker introduced Grant to his friend, John Rawlins, the County Attorney.

Following the outbreak of the Civil War, Parker sought a commission in the Union Army. While waiting for the appointment, he returned to the Tonawanda Reservation and farmed, which was not one of his primary interests. One of his Galena friends, Brigadier General John E. Smith, who commanded a division in Grant's army, wrote to the Army Personnel Office in Washington requesting that Parker be assigned as assistant adjutant general on his staff, noting that "he is well qualified for the position by education and experience." General Grant endorsed the request.

When Grant received no reply, he wrote to L. Thomas in Washington on June 25, 1863: "I am personally acquainted with Mr. Parker and I think [him] eminently qualified for the position. He is a full-blooded Indian but highly educated and very accomplished. He is a civil engineer of considerable eminence and served the government some years superintending the building of marine hospitals and custom houses on the upper Mississippi River." Parker was assigned the rank of captain of volunteers and joined Smith's division at Vicksburg, Mississippi, just after Confederate General Pemberton's surrender. In addition to his assistant adjutant general duties, Parker was assigned as division engineer of the Seventh Division, 17th Army Corps.

On September 18, 1863, Parker was reassigned as assistant adjutant general on General Grant's staff. His friend, John Rawlins from Galena, served on the staff in a similar capacity. While visiting Grant, Assistant Secretary of War Charles Dana, who had grown up in western New York, addressed Parker in the Seneca language. When Parker overcame his surprise, they had a long conversation.

Grant's staff moved to Chattanooga, where his army attacked Confederate positions on Lookout Mountain and Missionary Ridge. Parker described Grant's coolness under fire in the New York *Times*, January 17, 1864:

> It has been a matter of universal interest in this army that General Grant himself was not killed, and that no more accidents occurred to his staff, for the

General was always in the front, his staff with him of course, and perfectly heedless of the storm of hissing bullets and shells screaming around him.... Another feature in General Grant's personal movements is that he requires no escort beyond his staff, so regardless of danger is he.

Grant asked Parker to write the congratulatory victory letter to the army. Grant issued the order with few changes. Grant was promoted to lieutenant general and placed in command in the East. John Rawlins was promoted to brigadier general as Grant's chief of staff. On one occasion, Parker prevented the capture of Generals Grant and Meade and their staffs by questioning the direction in which they were headed and leading them back to Union lines. After the war, Confederate General Roger Prior told Parker of waiting to capture the two generals and their staffs until they changed directions and rode off.

On August 26, 1864, Parker was appointed military secretary with the rank of lieutenant colonel. He carried General Grant's papers, assisted him with his correspondence, and was at Grant's side for the remainder of the war.

By early 1865, Petersburg and Richmond had been taken by Union forces. On April 7, Grant corresponded with Lee, asking him to surrender the Army of Northern Virginia. Two days later, Lee asked for an interview to discuss terms of surrender. Grant asked Parker to write the reply to Lee arranging the meeting. Wilmer McLean offered his home in the village of Appomattox Court House as a place for the generals to meet.

Grant introduced his staff to Lee, who "shook hands with each in a most courteous, condescending and yet affable manner." When Lee shook hands with Parker, he said, "I am glad to see one real American here." Grant wrote his terms of surrender and reviewed them with Lee, who requested a few revisions. Grant asked Parker to make the changes. Colonel Bowers of Grant's staff began to write the official document in ink. He started to write the document several times, but, due either to being overwhelmed by the gravity of the occasion or from being tired from his ride from Burkeville earlier that day, he could not continue. Bowers turned to Parker and said: "Parker, you will have to write this, I can't do it." Parker wrote the copy using ink from the inkstand of Colonel Marshall, Lee's military secretary. Marshall wrote Lee's acceptance of the terms of surrender, using paper provided by Parker. Parker then wrote several orders for the Union Army regarding the surrender.

Grant's staff accompanied him to Washington to meet with President Lincoln on April 13. Parker showed the Red Jacket Medal to Lincoln, who "spoke feelingly of the associations it represents." Parker left later that day for leave in New York State. President Lincoln attended a play, "Our American Cousin," at Ford's Theatre, where he was assassinated by John Wilkes Booth. Parker was greatly saddened by the death of Lincoln. He said, "I am of a race that never forgives the murder of a friend." In late May, Parker, now a brevet colonel, returned to Washington for the grand review of the Union Armies, which took two full days.

Parker was appointed, on a part-time basis, to a commission dealing with Indian affairs. The commission met with Indian nations who had allied themselves with the Confederates to inform them that previous treaties with the Federal Government were invalid, and that new treaties would be renegotiated. Parker initiated numerous proposals that were well received. He remained on active duty in the army and was stationed at army headquarters in Washington.

In March 1866, Colonel Bowers, Grant's adjutant, was killed in an accident at West Point. Parker assumed Bowers's duties, and in July, when Grant became General-in-Chief of the Army, became Grant's aide-de-camp and was promoted to colonel and later to brevet brigadier general. He continued to serve on the Indian commission, making several more visits to the West.

In late 1867, the engagement of General Parker and Miss Minnie Orton Sackett was announced. Minnie was the attractive, White stepdaughter of Colonel William Sackett, commanding officer of the Ninth Cavalry, who had been killed near Trevilian Station, Virginia. Washington society was stirred by the announcement. Minnie said, "Some people thought I married the General because he was an Indian. Now I don't care for Indians—I married the General because I loved him."

Parker and Minnie were married on December 23, 1867. General Grant gave the bride away. After his marriage, Parker spent more time in Washington, where he and his wife attended receptions at the White House and at General Grant's home. Minnie was thought to "entertain as well as any lady in Washington." Parker supported Grant in his successful campaign for President in 1868.

Parker resigned from the Army as a brevet brigadier general, and, on April 13, 1869, Grant appointed him Commissioner of Indian Affairs in the Department of the Interior. He was responsible for the Government's relations with 300,000 Indians in the United States and its territories. Those relations were governed by 370 treaties. The Office of Indian Affairs had 38 clerks to assist Parker in the performance of his duties. Purchase of supplies for the Indians was one of the responsibilities of the office.

In 1870, Parker made arrangements for the purchase of supplies to keep promises to Indian nations prior to the belated approval by Congress of the appropriations bill. To avoid unrest by the Indians, he turned to a contractor whom he knew was reliable and could deliver the supplies on time. Parker considered the situation an emergency. Afterwards, however, he was questioned for not putting the order for supplies out for bid. The accusations were documented, and Parker found himself on trial in the House of Representatives. His friend Army Judge Advocate Norton Chipman defended him.

Parker was cleared of the charges, but his reputation was tarnished. He submitted his resignation "most respectfully but firmly" effective August 1, 1871. Grant told him that he had been "able and discreet" in managing Indian affairs, and that it had been done "in entire harmony" with his policy as President. Parker had instituted the Peace Policy with the Indians that was considered one of the accomplishments of Grant's administration.

Parker had no further interest in assignments with the Government. He and Minnie moved to Fairfield, Connecticut, where they had friends. He became a businessman and an investor, which included making investments in the Standard Oil Company. Some of his investments were not successful. He lost money with the collapse of Jay Cooke and Company and with the failure of the Freedmans' Bank. His most severe loss occurred when a bank cashier in New York, for whom he was a bondsman, embezzled money. Parker was asked to pay for the bond. He did not have to make it good, but, as later noted in the New York *Times* on September 1, 1895, Parker said, "I am a *man* and if the law does not compel me to pay, my honor does." His fortune was lost.

Parker went back to work. He found that in the 15 years since he had been an engineer, the field had changed considerably. Fortunately, one of his friends from his days in the Midwest, William F. Smith, president of the Board of Commissioners of the New York City Police Department, found a job for him.

Parker and Minnie moved to New York, where he worked for the Committee on Repairs and Supplies of the New York City Police Department. His job was to evaluate each requisition, determine its cost, and make a recommendation to the committee to accept or reject it. He prepared contracts and reviewed bills. Unfortunately, the pay was low, and he did not have much responsibility. He stayed in the job for 19 years, even though he was capable of handling considerably more responsibility.

Parker was active in the Grand Army of the Republic, the Society of Colonial Wars, and the Loyal Legion of the United States. His participation in these veterans' organizations took the place of the social aspects of his early Masonry activities. Parker suffered from rheumatism and diabetes in his later years. He worked for the New York City Police Department until three days before his death, after a series of strokes, on August 30, 1895. The medical examiner reported that he died of Bright's disease.

Parker's funeral service was at St. Paul's Episcopal Church in Fairfield, Connecticut. It was attended by Fred Grant, General Grant's son. General Grant had predeceased Parker. Members of the New York City Police Department, the Grand Army of the Republic, the Society of Colonial Wars, and the Loyal Legion of the United States attended the funeral. Ely Parker was buried in Oak Lawn Cemetery in Fairfield and then reinterred on January 27, 1897, in Forest Lawn Cemetery in Buffalo, near the grave of Red Jacket.

Minnie Parker was left with only a small pension as a veteran's widow. She sold her husband's personal belongings, his books, and the Red Jacket medal, which later was acquired by the Buffalo Historical Society.

In his biography of Ely Parker, Arthur Parker cited sculptor James E. Kelly's remarks to General Parker, while working on his bust:

> You are a man who has pierced the enemy's lines.
> You have torn yourself from one environment and
> made yourself the master of another. In this you have

done more for your people than any Indian who has ever lived. Had you remained with your people, and with your people alone, you might have been a Red Jacket, a Tecumseh, or a Brant, but by going out and away from them, you added to the honor that you already had and won equal, if not greater honors, among the White people. You proved what an Indian of capacity could be in the White man's world.

Red Jacket

Red Jacket was born at Canoga, south of Seneca Falls, in 1758. His father, Thadahwahnyeh, a Cayuga from the nearby village of Skoiyase, visited the Seneca village of Kanadesaga (Geneva) frequently. In fact, he had helped to build some of the longhouses at Kanadesaga. He met and fell in love with Blue Flower of the Wolf clan during his visits to the Seneca village. Although Thadahwahnyeh was not a Seneca, he was a member of the Turtle clan—the clan of the ruler of Kanadesaga.

The marriage was arranged by Thadahwahnyeh's and Blue Flower's mothers. The marriage proposal was announced in the council house, and the prospective bride and groom were reminded of the duties of marriage by the chief matron. After the ceremony and the wedding feast, the bride and groom moved into a lodge in Cayuga territory in the valley of Canoga Creek. The lodge was near a deep spring with an ample flow of water. Many bubbles came to the surface of the water, and the Cayugas believed that the spring had magical qualities. A New York State historic marker notes the site of the spring.

Within a year, Red Jacket was born at Canoga. The wife of Cayuga Chief Fish Carrier assisted at his birth. The proud parents traveled to Kanadesaga to show her haksaah (baby boy) to her relatives. He was not called Red Jacket until later in life. At the age of 10, he was welcomed into the Seneca Nation at the council house at Kanadesaga and given the name Otetiani, which means "always ready." Red Jacket hunted and fished with the other Indian boys and traveled widely around the region.

Red Jacket was a fast runner and was frequently used by the Senecas as a messenger. He was also employed as a messenger by the British during the Revolutionary War. For his services to them, the British gave him a scarlet jacket with fancy embroidery. It was a prized possession, and he wore it frequently. When a jacket wore out, the British provided him with a replacement.

Red Jacket was not a warrior. In fact, he did not take up arms until he was 29, when his territory was invaded; every Iroquois man had to defend his home and village. He was against war with the American colonists. He viewed them as neighbors and counseled neutrality and peace. Red Jacket said: "This quarrel does not belong to us, and it is best for us to take no part in it; we need not waste our blood to have it settled. If they fight us, we will fight them, but if they let us alone, we had better keep still." After the war, Chief Little Beard expressed his views: "Red Jacket was opposed to the war; he was always in favor of peace, and how much better it had been, had we listened to his advice."

Red Jacket was called a coward for his views. Pro-war advocates, such as Chief Joseph Brant of the Mohawks, considered him weak because he advocated peace. Brant told Red Jacket's wife, "Leave that man; leave him, lest your children have a coward for a father."

Red Jacket heard Chief Logan, son of Chief Shikellimus of the Cayuga Nation, speak and was moved by his style and the method of delivery of his speeches. Red Jacket would return from wandering in the woods and be asked what he had been doing. He would reply that "he had been playing Logan." Red Jacket developed his skills as an orator in council meetings. When his shortcomings as a warrior were raised, he responded, "I am an orator. I was born an orator." When he became a chief, the Senecas bestowed him with the name "Sagoyewatha," or "He keeps them awake."

In 1784, Red Jacket attended the treaty council at Fort Stanwix at present-day Rome, New York. General Lafayette was present at this council, and he was impressed by the eloquence of Red Jacket. Red Jacket was opposed to the Iroquois giving up the land that the commissioners requested, but he was overruled. Chief Cornplanter, the warrior, was the principal voice of the Six Nations of the Iroquois at the council.

In 1792, President Washington invited the leading Iroquois chiefs to Philadelphia to promote better understanding between Indians and the new government. Red Jacket and Farmer's Brother were among the 50 chiefs who met with Washington, Secretary of War Knox, and Colonel Pickering, the commissioner who negotiated with the Native Americans. Red Jacket spoke to the gathering, as noted by Arthur C.

Parker in *Red Jacket: Last of the Senecas*:

> All is in a measure now quieted. Peace is now bud-
> ding. But still there is some shaking among the orig-
> inal Americans toward the setting sun; and you of the
> 13 fires and the King of England know what our sit-
> uation is and the causes of this disturbance.... When
> you and the King made peace, he did not mention us
> and showed us no compassion, notwithstanding all
> he said to us and all we suffered. This has been the
> occasion of great sorrow and pain and great loss to
> us.... When you and he settled the peace between
> you, the great nations never asked us for a delegation
> to attend to our interests. Had he done this, a settle-
> ment of peace among the western nations might have
> been affected. But neglect of this has brought upon
> us great pain and trouble.... Our chain of peace has
> been broken.

Washington gave Red Jacket a large, oval silver medal as a token of his esteem and friendship. Engraved on the medal are the like-nesses of Red Jacket and President Washington sharing a peace pipe; a farmer and his oxen are in the background. The medal is now locat-ed at the Buffalo Historical Society Museum.

In 1794, a council between the 13 states and the Iroquois Confederacy was held in Canandaigua to discuss the Indians' concern about the loss of their lands. The United States was represented by Colonel Pickering and Thomas Morris, son of Robert Morris, financier of the Revolutionary War, attended. The Iroquois were rep-resented by 59 chiefs, including Cornplanter, Fish Carrier, and Red Jacket. As noted by J. Niles Hubbard in *Red Jacket and His People*, Thomas Morris observed:

> Red Jacket was ... of middle height, well-formed,
> with an intelligent countenance, and a fine eye, and
> was in all respects a fine looking man. He was the
> most graceful public speaker I have ever known; his
> manner was most dignified and easy. He was fluent,
> and at times witty and sarcastic. He was quick and
> ready at reply. He pitted himself against Colonel
> Pickering, whom he sometimes foiled in argument.

> The Colonel would sometimes become irritated and
> lose his temper; then Red Jacket would be delighted
> and show his dexterity in taking advantage of any
> unguarded assertion of the Colonel's. He felt a con-
> scious pride in the conviction that nature had done
> more for him than for his antagonist.

Red Jacket disagreed with the treaty proposed at Canandaigua,
but he eventually signed it so that the vote among the Iroquois would
appear to be unanimous. A year or two later, when Morris told Red
Jacket of Colonel Pickering's promotion from Postmaster General to
Secretary of War, Red Jacket said, "Ah! We began our public career
about the same time; he knew how to read and write; I did not, and
he has got ahead of me. If I had known how to read and write, I
should have got ahead of him."

In August 1797, Thomas Morris convened a council with the
leading chiefs of the Iroquois Confederacy at Big Tree (Geneseo)
concerning the sale of Indian lands in western New York. In the
spring of 1791, Robert Morris had purchased the pre-emptive right to
the lands in western New York other than those lands involved in the
Phelps-Gorham Purchase. He promised to survey the entire tract and
to satisfy the Indian title. Robert Morris commissioned his son to represent him in obtaining the consent of the Iroquois to sell their land.

Cornplanter, Farmer's Brother, Little Beard, Little Billy, and Red
Jacket conducted most of the discussions for the Iroquois. Red Jacket,
as the principal spokesman, told Morris the Indians' view of selling
their lands: "We are not convinced that it is best to dispose of them at
any price." Morris asked, "But what value can they be to you as they
now are, any further than the consciousness that you own them?" As
noted by Arthur C. Parker in *Red Jacket: Last of the Senecas*, Red
Jacket responded:

> To own such a territory means everything to us. It
> raises us in our own estimation; it creates in our
> bosoms a proud feeling which elevates us as a
> nation. Observe the difference between the estima-
> tion in which a Seneca and an Oneida are held. We
> are courted, while the Oneidas are considered a
> degraded people fit only to make brooms and bas-
> kets. Why this difference? It is because the Senecas

Red Jacket Statue, Red Jacket Park, Penn Yan

are known as proprietors of a broad domain, while
the Oneidas are cooped up in a narrow space.

While Red Jacket was still standing, one of the Senecas said,
"He's a coward." Red Jacket replied: "Yes, I am a coward." Then he
waved his hand around in a semicircle pointing to the beautiful country that surrounded them. He added: "Assure me that you can create
lands like these, which the Great Spirit has made for his red children,
so that you can give us lands like them in return, and I will be brave.
Until then, I am a coward; I dare not sell these lands." Again,
although Red Jacket objected to the selling of Iroquois lands, he
eventually signed the agreement with the other chiefs.

Strain had existed between Cornplanter and Red Jacket from the
time of their youth. At a time when Cornplanter was losing influence
in the Confederacy, he tried to soften his loss of influence by cutting
down one of his rivals, Red Jacket. Cornplanter convinced his brother, Handsome Lake the prophet, to accuse Red Jacket of witchcraft.
A board of judges met, heard the charges against Red Jacket, and
charged him with sorcery. If found guilty, he could have been punished by death. The tribal court met at Buffalo Creek; the judges listened to the slanderous charges.

Red Jacket conducted his own defense. He began by looking each
accuser in the eye and saying, "So that is the best you can do with
lies!" He analyzed the character of his accusers, citing instance after
instance that clearly showed their prejudice. He noted deed after deed
in which his accusers had been dishonest or deceitful and had acted
contrary to the best interests of the Senecas.

He concluded by saying, "Cornplanter, you're a cheat! You've
heard me; and the prophet is an impostor." The judges returned with
a verdict of not guilty. Cornplanter retired to his lodge and concerned
himself with improving the living conditions of his people; he was no
longer a force as a leader.

On January 20, 1830, Red Jacket died at the Buffalo Creek
Reservation as he approached 80 years of age. On his death bed, he
said to his wife, "I am going to die. I shall never leave this house
alive. I wish to thank you for your kindness to me. You have loved
me. You have always prepared my food, and taken care of my clothes,
and been patient with me.... I should like to live longer for your sake.
I meant to build you a new house and make you comfortable in it, but

Red Jacket Memorial, Canoga

it is now too late." He had at his side a bottle of water from the spring at Canoga that he thought would assure him a safe passage to the next world.

Red Jacket always spoke in the Seneca language and insisted that an interpreter translate his speeches into English. He did not believe in the Christian faith. In fact, he had left his wife when she converted to Christianity. However, he recognized the error of his ways and returned to her.

On his deathbed, he told her: "I am sorry I left you because of your new religion. I am convinced it is a good religion and has made you a better woman and wish you to persevere in it."

Colonel William Jones of Geneseo, son of pioneer Horatio Jones, observed of Red Jacket: "For the great men of our own and of other times have become so by education; but Red Jacket was as nature made him. Had he enjoyed their advantages, he would have surpassed them, since it can hardly be supposed that they, without these, would have equaled him." Jones maintained that Red Jacket's talents "were among the noblest that nature ever conferred upon man."

Kateri Tekakwitha, "Lily of the Mohawks"

Kateri (Katherine) Tekakwitha was born in 1656 in the triple-palisaded Mohawk village of Ossernenon, now Auriesville, west of Amsterdam. The Mohawks were known for the fierceness of their warriors. The Mohawk Nation had three clans: Turtle, Bear, and Wolf. Kateri's village was a Turtle Clan village and her father was a chief of the Turtle Clan. Her mother was an Algonquin who had been captured by the Mohawks at Three Rivers, near Quebec. Her marriage to the chief saved her from death or slavery. She was a convert to Christianity.

In 1660, Kateri's village had an outbreak of smallpox, and her father, mother, and younger brother died in the epidemic. Four-year-old Kateri was afflicted with poor eyesight and was left with a pock-marked face. She was adopted by her father's brother, a village chief. The Turtle clan relocated a mile west of Ossernenon between Auries Creek and the Mohawk River. The new village was called "Gandawague," "the rapids." At that time, Kateri was given the name "Tekakwitha," "She who puts things in order." By adopting Kateri, her uncle gained a young worker in a family in which his wife and sister were getting on in years.

Gandawague had 25 longhouses, each sheltering 10 to 20 families depending on the size of the dwelling. Each longhouse had several hearths with smokeholes above them in the roof. Kateri carried water from the spring, gathered firewood, and worked in the fields tending the beans, corn, and squash. She learned to cook, sew, embroider, and weave. Her aunts were impressed with her mastery of these tasks and with her industry.

When she was eight, Kateri was promised in marriage to a young boy chosen by her aunts, according to traditional practice. It is likely that she did not even know of the arrangement. Her uncle looked forward to adding a hunter and warrior to his household.

Truce between the French in their forts along the St. Lawrence River and the Mohawks was always uneasy, and treaties were frequently broken by Indian raids. In *Old Regime in Canada,* Francis Parkman notes that "they approach like foxes, attack like lions, and disappear like birds." In 1666, when Kateri was 10, French General de Tracy left Quebec with over 1,000 French Canadian soldiers and 100 Algonquin and Huron warriors to attack and destroy the Mohawk villages.

The Turtle Clan at Gandawaque was caught by surprise and fled westward to the triple-palisaded capital village of the Mohawks at Tionnontoguen. The Bear Clan also fled to the Wolf Clan village of Tionnontoguen from their village at Andagaron. Soon they heard de Tracy's cannon, which helped the French overwhelm the Mohawks armed with rifles obtained from the Dutch. The Mohawks fled, and de Tracy's men burned the village and destroyed crops in the field and stored food. Many Mohawks did not live through the cold and hunger of that winter. Kateri was one of the fortunate ones to survive, living on berries, roots, and nuts.

The following spring, Mohawks traveled to Quebec to sign a peace treaty with the French that lasted 18 years. The other Iroquois nations also made peace with the French Canadians. The Turtle Clan built a new village, Caughnawaga, near the confluence of Cayudutta Creek and the Mohawk River. Caughnawaga, which like Gandawague meant "the rapids," was named for the rapids of Cayudutta Creek.

Three Jesuit priests, Fathers Bruyas, Fremin, and Pierron, returned to the Turtle Clan village in Mohawk Valley from Quebec with the Mohawk negotiators. They were guests of Kateri's uncle for three days. She prepared and served their food. She was impressed with the gentle manner of the "Blackrobes."

Kateri was an intelligent, sensitive young woman who felt that something was missing in her life. She was attracted to the beliefs of the Blackrobes, partly because her mother had been a Christian. The priests observed her eager manner and quickness to comprehend. A fourth Jesuit priest who was associated with her later, Father Cholenec, noted in his biography, *Katherine Tekakwitha*:

> The modesty and sweetness with which she acquitted herself of her duty to them touched her new guests, while on her part she was struck with their affable manners, their regularity in prayer, and the other exercises into which they divided their day. God even then disposed her to the grace of Baptism, for which she would have asked, if the missionaries had remained longer in her village.

The visit of the Jesuit priests gave new focus to the spiritual development of the 11-year-old Kateri. She began to think that there might be answers to many of her questions. Somehow, life among the Mohawks did not seem to her a full life, a complete life. Father Pierron returned to their village as Christian minister to the Turtle Clan. He was not particularly welcomed, but he was not treated harshly. The chief viewed his presence as a requirement of the peace treaty with the French Canadians.

Father Pierron built a small chapel dedicated to St. Peter to begin his mission. Although he could not speak the Mohawk language, he managed to instruct the Turtle Clan using pictures and games as aids in illustrating religious principles. The teachings of Father Pierron and his replacement, Father Boniface, were effective, and they attracted many villagers to Catholicism. Kateri's uncle would not permit her to convert to Christianity; however, the early thoughts of a new religion for her began when she heard the Indian children singing the "Te Deum."

Although Kateri became known for her needlework, she did not make fancy clothes for herself. She was inherently modest. Her aunts thought that she should dress less conservatively to attract a brave eligible for marriage. She was firm in telling her aunts that she did not want to discuss the subject of marriage. Her rejection of marriage disgraced her in the eyes of her uncle and her aunts. She was given many menial tasks.

Father Boniface was replaced by Father de Lamberville, a dedicated, energetic priest who ministered to the Bear Clan at Andagaron. Furthermore, he had learned the Mohawk language to assist him in his missionary work with the Iroquois. Kateri hesitated to approach the priest to tell him of her interest in Christianity because of her uncle's strong opposition. She had no close friend to convey her sentiments to Father de Lamberville. Anastasia, "Tegonhatsihongo," a Christian convert who been a friend of Kateri's mother, had moved to the La Prairie Mission in Canada, taking with her the young woman Kateri had considered to be her adopted sister.

At the age of 12, Kateri injured her foot while felling a tree. For a while, she could not work in the fields, fetch water, or gather firewood. When Father de Lamberville visited her at her cabin one day, she told him of her feelings about Christianity, her desire for religious instruction, and her wish to be baptized. Father de Lamberville reminded her of the difficulties that she would face, but she was determined to proceed. In *The Jesuit Relations and Allied Documents*, Father Charlevoix describes Father de Lamberville's perception of Kateri's revelations:

> The energy with which she spoke, the courage she displayed, a certain modest but resolute air that lighted up her countenance, at once told the missionary that this new proselyte would not be an ordinary Christian. He accordingly carefully taught her many things, which he did not explain to all preparing for Baptism.

As soon as her foot healed, Kateri attended morning and evening prayers at the chapel. She was intelligent and learned quickly. It seemed to her that a powerful light had begun to shine upon her. Father de Lamberville questioned her family and fellow villagers to investigate her character prior to her baptism. No one, including her uncle, spoke out against her. Father de Lamberville perceived Kateri's potential for leadership among her people and among Christians, generally. He wanted to make Kateri's baptism a special occasion so he chose to administer the sacrament to her on Easter Sunday 1676.

Statue of Kateri Tekakwitha, Auriesville

Father de Lamberville gave his candidate for baptism the name Katherine, meaning "pure." He poured baptismal water on her head as he said, "Katherine, I baptize you in the name of the Father, the Son, and the Holy Ghost. Amen." The 20-year-old Mohawk maiden was ready to continue her spiritual journey. Kateri did her chores for the Mohawk community, but she refused to work on Sundays and holy days. Therefore, she was denied food on those days of rest, because she had not worked for it.

Kateri became the target of taunts and jeers from non-Christian members of the village. People tend to fear or suspect that which they do not understand. One day, a drunken young Mohawk entered her cabin and threatened her with a tomahawk, possibly because she had rejected all suitors. He expected her to cry out or shake under the weapon positioned over head. Instead, she stood before him with her head slightly bowed, displaying courage and faith in God. The young man was surprised by her demeanor and lowered the tomahawk before walking away, unnerved by her display of strength.

Kateri continued to press Father de Lamberville for additional religious duties and for increased demands to be placed upon her spiritually. He knew of her interest in La Prairie, where her friend Anastasia and her adopted sister and her husband were leading Christian lives with the Jesuits. The La Prairie Mission, now called St. Francis Xavier Mission at Sault Ste. Louis, had been moved up the St. Lawrence River to where the Lachine Rapids enter the river. It was also called Caughnawaga, the same name as the old village on the Mohawk River.

Father de Lamberville knew that for Kateri to continue to grow spiritually, she needed a place like Caughnawaga. However, Kateri could not just leave her village. She would have to go secretly, under the protection of companions willing to risk capture by men sent by her uncle to return her to the village.

In the fall of 1677, three Indians, including the husband of Kateri's adopted sister, traveled up the Mohawk River by canoe to Caughnawaga. Hot Ashes was the leader of the expedition to broadcast the word of the Christian faith and to tell the Iroquois of the St. Francis Xavier Mission in Canada. Kateri was moved by Hot Ashes's description of the Canadian Mission. She told Father de Lamberville of her interest in going to Sault Ste. Louis. He agreed that it would be a beneficial move for her.

Hot Ashes's canoe could hold only three people so he proceeded on foot, giving up his place in the canoe to Kateri. When her uncle was away at Fort Orange (Albany) negotiating with the English, Kateri went with her adopted sister's husband and his Huron companion. She knew that the trip through swamps and woods would be difficult. Her parting with Father de Lamberville was emotional. He gave her a letter to Father Cholenec at the St. Francis Xavier Mission that is documented in *The Jesuit Relations and Allied Documents:* "Katherine Tegakouita [sic] is going to live at the Sault. Will you kindly undertake to direct her? You will soon know what a treasure we have sent you. Guard it well then! May it profit in your hands, for the glory of God and the salvation of a soul that certainly is very dear to Him."

When her uncle returned from Albany, he loaded his rifle with three bullets and set out to catch up with Kateri and her two companions. Father Cholenec documented the incident in *Katherine Tekakwitha* in 1696:

> They saw him coming from afar, and as they were doubtful of his plans, they hid Katherine in the woods, while the others sat down by the road as if to eat. Coming upon them, he asked them very abruptly where his niece was. They answered that they had seen her in the village, and that they could not tell him anything else about her; whereupon the old man, God doubtless wishing it to be so, turned back without any further effort to find her.

They resumed their journey and reached the St. Francis Xavier Mission in the autumn of 1677.

The travelers were greeted enthusiastically, and Kateri moved into the lodge that Anastasia shared with Kateri's adopted sister and her husband. Kateri was welcomed by the villagers as she began her new life. She was received warmly by Father Cholenec and the other Jesuits, Fathers Fremin and Chauchetiere. They inspired her in a spiritual environment that was very different from life with the Mohawks.

Kateri began her day at 4:00 a.m. praying in the chapel. She attended mass at sunrise and visited the chapel to pray several times during the day for her salvation and that of all those of the Turtle

Clan. Sundays and holy days were the peaks of Kateri's existence. She said the rosary frequently and attended vespers daily. Her devotion was obvious to the priests. They observed her piety as she quickly learned about the Creed, the Ten Commandments, and the lives of the saints.

Father Cholenec shortened the usual length of time to prepare for First Communion and announced that Kateri would receive the sacrament on Christmas Day. She was humble, but she was ready to receive the Holy Eucharist for the first time. After receiving the sacrament, she seemed changed. As documented in *The Jesuit Relations and Allied Documents,* Father Cholenec wrote: "Our Lord knew what passed between Himself and His dear spouse during her First Communion. All that we can say is from that day forward, she appeared different to us, because she remained so full of God and love of Him."

Since Kateri was fed and cared for by the people of the village, she had an obligation to help in raising crops and in gathering food. She joined her adopted sister and her husband on the hunting expedition that winter. She missed attending chapel; however, at the end of the day around the campfire, she led members of the expedition in singing hymns and in telling stories about the lives of the saints.

Upon her return from the hunt, Kateri was struck on the head by a falling limb and knocked unconscious. When she regained consciousness, she thanked the Lord for her recovery. She felt that God had saved her life to permit her to continue to atone for her sins.

Father Cholenec was impressed with the fervor of Kateri's beliefs and the seriousness with which she performed her religious duties. He decided that she was ready to join the Holy Family, although that was usually reserved for older members of the church who had expressed their faith over a long period of time. The villagers devoted to their religion agreed with the Jesuits that this young woman was extraordinary. On Easter Sunday 1678, Kateri received her Second Communion and joined the Confraternity of the Holy Family. This bound her more strongly to the Church and strengthened her relationship with Jesus Christ.

Kateri spent much of her time in meditation; nevertheless, she had close friends in the village. One of her friends was Marie Theresa Tegaiaguenta, a young widow. Kateri and Maria Theresa traveled to Montreal to visit the Sisters of the Congregation of Notre Dame and the Sisters of the Hotel-Dieu. The young women were impressed with nuns dressed in black and white who taught the children and attended the sick. Upon their return to Caughnawaga, they consulted with an older woman, Marie Skarichions, about forming a monastic organization similar to the ones that Kateri and Marie Theresa had seen in Montreal. They proposed locating their lodge on Heron Island in the river. Father Cholenec rejected their proposal for practical reasons. Crossing the rapids to get to the Island was dangerous, and he asked how they would obtain their food. In the rough society in which they lived, he asked who would protect them if they lived alone on the Island.

Kateri was pressured by her adopted sister to marry, according to Iroquois custom. The sister obtained the backing of Anastasia, and soon both older women were encouraging Kateri to marry. They presented their case to Father Cholenec, who also listened to Kateri's side of the story. Kateri told the Jesuit that she was ready to take a vow of chastity. Father Cholenec made the necessary preparations and documented the occasion in *The Jesuit Relations and Associated Documents*:

> It was the Feast of the Annunciation, March 25, 1679, at eight o'clock in the morning, when a moment after Jesus Christ gave himself to her in Communion, Katherine Tegakouita (sic) wholly gave herself to Him, and renouncing marriage forever, promised him perpetual virginity. With a heart aglow with love, she implored Him to be her Spouse and to accept her as His bride.

Kateri's health had never been strong, and the punishment that she gave her body to atone for her sins weakened her. She burned her legs with firebrands and placed burning coals between her toes. She wore a spiked iron girdle and asked Marie Theresa to scourge her bare shoulders. She slept on thorns until Maria Theresa told Father Cholenec of Kateri's "penances." She fasted frequently, which reduced her strength even further. She fell ill, and it became obvious that she was not going to recover. She was administered the Last Rites of the Church, and on April 17, 1680, during Holy Week, Kateri died.

Father Cholenec noted that "a great change took place in her appearance after her death where her face, pitted with smallpox scars, became almost instantly very beautiful and fair." Several nights later, Anastasia was awakened by a voice that called "mother" and asked her to look up. Anastasia saw a body engulfed in light holding a cross and recognized Kateri's face. Kateri spoke briefly and disappeared.

Kateri next appeared to Father Chauchetiere. He saw her right a church that had been turned upside down—to her left were some Indians burning at the stake. Later, the Mission church was in fact overturned during a violent storm, and Iroquois raiders captured an Indian man and two women and subsequently burned them at the stake. Kateri appeared to Father Chauchetiere a second time to ask him to paint a portrait of her holding a cross in her hand. He honored this request in 1681. She appeared to Father Chauchetiere a third time in 1682. She also appeared to her friend Marie Theresa Tegaiaguenta.

Many "miraculous instances" have been attributed to Kateri, including:

- A woman dying of cancer made an overnight recovery after praying while holding a small piece of cloth that had touched Kateri's bones.
- A man from Three Rivers with gangrene in his foot was able to wear both of his shoes on the fifth day of a novena, a nine-day prayer, to Kateri.
- A cripple prayed to Kateri at the Caughnawaga Mission church and was able to walk away without his crutches.

In 1939, the Congregation of Rites of the Catholic Church accepted the Cause for Canonization of Kateri Tekakwitha. In 1943, she was venerated by Pope Pius XII because she had practiced all of the "heroic virtues": faith, hope, charity, and chastity. In 1980, Pope John Paul II beatified the Lily of the Mohawks. Normally, four miracles are required for beatification, except for founders of religious orders. Kateri had proposed a new order of nuns on Heron Island, but the Jesuits rejected her proposal. She needs one more miracle for Canonization. If this occurs, she would be the first Native American to become a Saint.

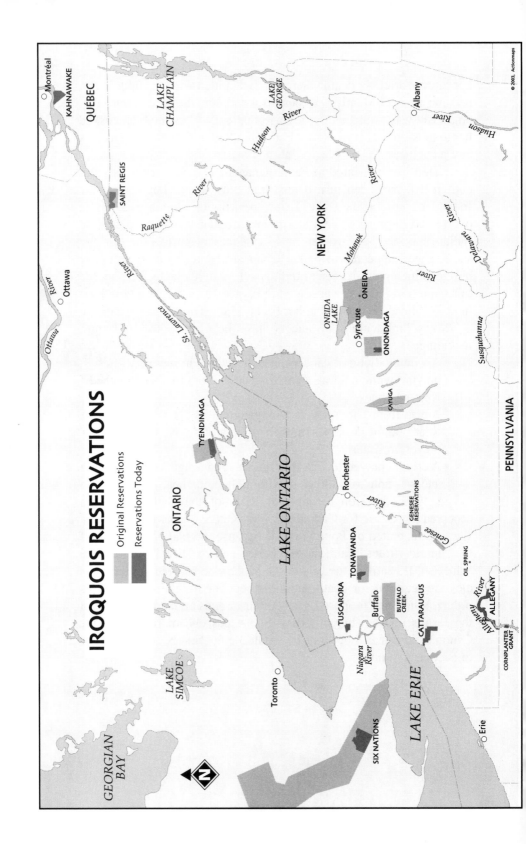

IROQUOIS RESERVATIONS

Original Reservations
Reservations Today

© 2003, Actionmaps

Turning Stone Casino of the Oneida Nation, Verona

EPILOGUE

"Although members of the Confederacy have lost much land, they have never lost their spirit. Population estimates vary, but some sources indicate that between 40,000 and 60,000 Confederacy members live in the United States, and a similar number live in Canada [1990s]. And today the members of the Confederacy who gave friendship and counsel to America's founders are beginning to be recognized as heroes of democracy."

Evelyn Wolfson, *The Iroquois People of the Northeast*

HISTORY

Twentieth and Twenty-first Centuries

In 1924, U.S. citizenship was conferred on all Native Americans living in the United States. The Iroquois Nations traditionally had rejected American citizenship because they thought that it compromised their sovereignty. When they traveled abroad, they carried an Iroquois passport. In 1928, the U.S. Congress passed legislation to allow uninterrupted passage by Native Americans across the U.S. / Canada border. In 1932, children at the Tuscarora Reservation became the first Native Americans integrated into the local public school system.

The Indian Reorganization Act of 1934 provided for tribal self-government and ended the policy of allotting tribal lands to individuals. The act modified the relationship between Native Americans and the Federal Government. William Dudley describes the act in *Native Americans*: "An act to conserve and develop Indian lands and resources; to extend to Indians the right to form business and other organization; to establish a credit system for Indians; to grant certain rights of home rule to Indians; to provide for vocational education for Indians; and for other purposes."

In 1987, the U.S. Supreme Court ruled to protect the rights of Indians to have gaming on their reservations in states that do not forbid it. The rights of reservations were defined further by the Indian Gaming Regulatory Act of 1988. By 1993, 124 Indian casinos were operating in 24 states. By 2002, 290 Indian casinos in the United States reported a combined annual revenue of $12.7 billion. An early Iroquois casino was one on the Mohawk reservation at St. Regis; another was Turning Stone Casino of the Oneida Nation at Oneida.

Senecas

In 1941, the U.S. Congress authorized a plan to build a flood control dam on the Allegheny River at Kinzua. The reservoir behind this dam would flood one third of the Allegany Reservation. Planning for the dam resumed in 1956. The Seneca Nation, supported by Quakers, contested the project and, when they could not stop it, asked for compensation.

Over 9,000 acres of the best Seneca land was to be taken. Since

12,000 acres of the reservation were mountainous, the nation was left with only 2,300 acres on which it was practical to build. Over 130 families had to relocate outside of the reservoir area. Sacred burial grounds had to be dug up and moved. Ultimately, the Senecas were paid $15 million in direct damages and rehabilitation costs. In 1965, the Longhouse fire had to be moved from the Coldspring longhouse, site of Handsome Lake's revelations, to Steamburg.

In the 1950s, a section of the New York State Thruway was built through the Cattaraugus Reservation. Later, the State of New York expanded the Southern Tier Expressway, Route 17, now I-86, through the Allegany Reservation. The Senecas demanded compensation. If compensation payments were not timely, the Senecas closed roads and stopped traffic.

In 2002, New York State approved the establishment of three Seneca casinos in western New York. In 2002-03, the Seneca Nation renovated the Niagara Falls, New York, Convention Center and opened the Seneca Niagara Casino. The master plan for the 55-acre site includes a nightclub-style showroom, two hotels, a parking garage, restaurants including a 350-seat dining hall and a 150-seat bistro and pub, and separate gaming areas for high-stakes gamblers and nonsmokers.

Cayugas

In 1980, the Cayuga Indian Nation of New York filed suit in federal court in Syracuse against New York State, Seneca and Cayuga Counties, and 7,000 landowners seeking $350 million in damages and ownership of 64,015 acres of land on both sides of Cayuga Lake. These were the lands that the Cayuga Nation sold to New York State in 1795 and 1807. The 100-square mile tract is comprised of 42,000 acres in Cayuga County and 22,000 acres in Seneca County near Seneca Falls. In 1991, after rejecting previous rulings by the defendants, U.S. District Judge Neal P. McCurn found the defendants liable. New York State maintained that it cannot be sued. The following year, the U.S. Justice Department also sided with the Cayuga Nation.

In 1999, Judge McCurn ruled that New York State can be sued; however, he also held that landowners cannot be forced from property to which they have deeds. On February 17, 2000, the jury recommended a preliminary award to the Cayuga Nation of $36.9 million. Appraisers for New York State had suggested $51 million; the Cayuga Nation had initially asked for $350 million. The ruling was appealed.

Onondagas

The Onondaga Nation maintains a reservation of 6,100 acres, just south of Syracuse, off I-81 Expressway. Most Onondagas are Christians and attend Episcopal, Methodist, or Wesleyan churches on the reservation or in Syracuse. By the 1970s, about a quarter of them were followers of Handsome Lake. Referred to as members of the "Council House," they performed traditional Iroquois ceremonies. The reservation is governed by a council of hereditary chiefs, which conducts the economic, political, religious, and social affairs of the nation.

An elementary school, the Onondaga Council House, and a large, comprehensive community center are located on the reservation. The Onondaga Nation maintains its own volunteer fire department. From 1970 to 1974, Onondagas prevented New York State from using reservation land to widen a highway and later negotiated the return of historic wampum belts from New York State.

On October 13, 1989, 12 Iroquois wampum belts that had been turned over to the New York State Museum for safekeeping were returned to the Onondagas in a ceremony in Albany. Included among the 12 were the four major belts: the Washington Covenant belt, the Wing or Dust Fan Belt, the Thadodaho belt, and the Hiawatha belt.

Tuscaroras

In the late 1950s, 1,383 acres, over one fifth of the Tuscarora Reservation, were taken over by the New York Power Authority to build a storage reservoir for a hydroelectric generation plant. Tuscaroras manned barricades to prevent surveys from being made and fought the acquisition in the courts. Bulldozing was stopped when 30 Tuscarora bulldozer operators stepped down from their equipment.

In 1959, the U.S. District Court of Appeals forwarded the case to the Federal Power Commission and the Federal courts, which ordered the New York Power Authority to desist. However, in 1960, the U.S. Supreme Court overturned the Federal Power Commission ruling in favor of the Tuscaroras, and construction of the Niagara Power Plant proceeded.

The Tuscaroras maintain a community center on Route 31 west of Lockport. The Joseph Jacobs Museum, a gem of a museum with artifacts, sculptures, paintings, and photographs, adjoins the community center.

Oneidas

Interest in farming declined in the early 1900s, and many Oneidas began to earn wages. By 1908 in Wisconsin, most Oneida land was subjected to town and county taxes. Foreclosures and sales of land to pay back taxes became prevalent. In 1925, only several hundred acres were owned by Oneidas. Many Oneidas worked as laborers on farms owned by others or in factories. Many moved to Green Bay and Milwaukee in search of jobs. By 1972, Oneidas owned 2,200 acres of land in Wisconsin. Most of this had been purchased for them by the U.S. Government through the Indian Reorganization Act.

By 1972, fewer than 2,000 Oneidas were associated with the Thames (London, Ontario) Reservation, only 1,200 of whom lived on the reservation. Most worked in the nearby municipalities of London or St. Thomas. Few Oneidas farmed their own land; many leased their land to White farmers. Anglicans and Methodists are still predominant, although some are Baptists, and a few practice the New Religion of Handsome Lake.

Several hundred Oneidas remained in New York State after the relocations to Wisconsin and Canada. By 1972, 600 Oneidas lived near Oneida, New York, or on the Onondaga Reservation near Syracuse. During the 1990s, the Oneida Nation opened the Turning Stone Casino near Oneida, which has a conference center, three golf courses, seven restaurants, and offers world-class entertainment.

Mohawks

The Caughnawaga Reservation is on the south shore of the St. Lawrence River, nine miles upriver from Montreal, just above the Lachine Rapids. The small reservation, which consists of farmland and timber, borders the river for eight miles and is four-miles wide at its widest point. Few of the Mohawks are farmers; they lease their farmland to French-Canadian farmers. The village of Caughnawaga is on the highway from Montreal to New York State.

St. Francis Xavier's church, a Jesuit mission, is the largest church in the village. The church attracts tourists because it houses the bones of Kateri Tekakwitha, Lily of the Mohawks, who died in 1680 at the age of 24. Her bones lie on a silk cushion in a glass-topped chest. People make pilgrimages to pray before them in hopes of curing their afflictions. The Church claims that pilgrims have been cured of diseases, including cancer, by Kateri Tekakwitha's intercession.

In 1886, the Dominion Bridge Company (DBC), began to build a railroad bridge across the St. Lawrence River from Lachine on the north shore to the Caughnawaga Reservation on the south shore. To obtain the right to build a bridge abutment on reservation land, the Canadian Pacific Railroad promised to hire Mohawks on the construction crew. The Mohawks began as laborers, but it was soon observed that they had no fear of heights. They excelled at high steelwork, which was the highest-paid construction speciality.

Fifty Mohawks worked on the next construction project for the DBC, the Soo Bridge spanning two canals and a river between Sault Ste. Marie, Ontario, to Sault Ste. Marie, Michigan. By 1907, 70 Mohawks were bridgemen.

On August 29, 1907, a span collapsed during the construction of the Quebec Bridge across the St. Lawrence River, nine miles north of Quebec City. Thirty-three of the 96 men killed were from the Caughnawaga Reservation. Instead of turning them away from the occupation, it motivated them to continue because the dangerous nature of the work was now widely known. Young Mohawks looked up to the bridgemen.

Early in the 20th century, when many of New York's skyscrapers were being built, Mohawks from the Caughnawaga Reservation in the Province of Quebec did much of the high steelwork. About 650 of the 3,000 on the reservation moved from building site to building site to erect the steel framework for bridges and high-rise buildings. Caughnawaga settlements were established in major cities, including Brooklyn, Buffalo, and Detroit. The largest settlement was in the North Gowanus section of Brooklyn. By the 1990s, 800 Mohawks were doing high steelwork.

In 1915, John Diablo and three other Caughnawaga Mohawks worked on the Hell Gate Bridge in New York City. Diablo, a highly skilled worker, stepped off a scaffold and was drowned in a freak accident. The other three Mohawks took his body back to the reservation and did not return to the job.

In 1926, four high-steel gangs came to New York to work on three buildings, including the Graybar Building. In 1928, three Caughnawaga teams worked on the George Washington Bridge, and in the early 1930s, seven gangs worked on the construction of Rockefeller Center.

Subsequently, Caughnawaga gangs worked on many New York projects, including the R.C.A. Building, the Empire State Building, the Chrysler Building, the Triborough Bridge, the Henry Hudson Bridge, the Bronx-Whitestone Bridge, the Pulaski Skyway, the West Side Highway, and the Waldorf-Astoria Hotel. Caughnawagas also worked on the Golden Gate Bridge in San Francisco, California, and on construction projects in 16 other states.

Modern Caughnawaga Mohawks are still active in the construction industry, moving from job to job, from city to city. They take pride in their work, which they recognize as a tough and hazardous profession. They have been asked what motivates them, and if their wanderlust is inherited from their wandering ancestors. The current generation explains their motivation to work on high steel; it is because "they are not afraid to die."

Construction of the St. Lawrence Seaway affected the St. Regis (Akwesasne) Reservation near Ogdensburg and the Caughnawaga (Kahnawake) Reservation near Montreal. The St. Regis Reservation is partly in New York State and partly in Ontario and Quebec Provinces. The St. Lawrence Seaway passes though the St. Regis Reservation. In the 1950s, the U.S. Government took 88 acres of Racquette Point and all of Barnhardt Island to construct a dam. The Canadian Government expropriated Mohawk land for customs facilities and the construction of a bridge.

In the late 1950s, the St. Lawrence Seaway Authority used 1,260 acres of the Kahnawake Reservation for the construction of a canal to bypass the Lachine Rapids. Part of a 200-year-old village was sacrificed. The modest monetary compensation was less than the market value of land in the area. Mohawks complained to the United Nations Human Rights Commission, which took no action.

In 1969, Mohawks blockaded the bridge on their reservation to force the Canadian Government to recognize the 1794 Jay Treaty that permitted all Native Americans to move unrestricted across the United States-Canada international boundary. In 1970, Mohawks occupied two islands in the St. Lawrence River to force the Canadian Government to recognize that they were part of the St. Regis Reservation.

* * *

Ye say they all have passed away,
That noble race and brave,
That their light canoes have vanished
From off the crested wave;
That 'mid the forest where they roamed
There rings no hunters' shout;
But their name is on your waters,
Ye may not wash it out.

Ye say their ... cabins
That clustered o'er the vale,
Have fled like withered leaves
Before the Autumn's gale;
But their memory liveth on your hills,
Their baptism on your shore;
Your everlasting rivers speak
Their dialect of yore.

From "Indian Names" by Lydia Huntley Sigourney

BIBLIOGRAPHY

Abrams, George H. J. *The Seneca People*. Phoenix: Indian Tribal Series, 1976.

Armstrong, William H. *Warrior in Two Camps: Ely S. Parker, Union General and Seneca Chief*. Syracuse: Syracuse UP, 1978.

Beale, Irene A. *Genesee Country Senecas*. Geneseo, NY: Chestnut Hill Press, 1992.

—. *Genesee Valley Events: 1668-1986*. Geneseo, NY: Chestnut Hill Press, 1986.

Beauchamp, William M. *A History of the New York Iroquois*. Bulletin 78. Albany: New York State Museum, 1905.

—. Iroquois Folk Lore. Port Washington, NY: Ira J. Friedman, 1965.

Bjornlund, Lydia. *The Iroquois*. San Diego: Lucent Books, 2001.

Bloomfield, J. K. *The Oneidas*. New York: Alden Brothers, 1907.

Bonvillan, Nancy. *The Mohawk*. New York: Chelsea House, 1992.

Britt, Albert. *Great Indian Chiefs*. New York: McGraw-Hill, 1938.

Bruchac, Joseph. *Iroquois Stories: Heroes and Heroines, Monsters and Magic*. Trumansburg, NY: Crossing Press, 1985.

Buehrie, Marie Cecilia. *Kateri of the Mohawk*. New York: All Saints Press, 1966.

Canfield, William W. *The Legends of the Iroquois Told by "The Cornplanter."* Port Washington, NY: Ira J. Friedman, 1971.

Carmer, Carl. *Dark Trees to the Wind: A Cycle of York State Years*. New York: W. S. Lowe Associates, 1949.

—. *Listen for a Lonesome Drum: A York State Chronicle*. New York: Farrar & Rinehart, 1936.

Chalmers, Harvey and Ethel Brant Monture. *Joseph Brant: Mohawk*. East Lansing: Michigan State UP, 1955.

Clark, Joshua V. *Onondaga: Or Reminiscences of Earlier and Later Times*. Syracuse: Stoddard and Babcock, 1849.

Colden, Cadwallader. *The History of the Five Nations Depending on the Province of New York in America*. Ithaca: Great Seal Books, 1958.

Converse, H. M. *Myths and Legends of the New York State Iroquois*, Bulletin 125. Albany: New York State Museum, 1981.

Cornplanter, Jesse J. *Legends of the Longhouse*. Philadelphia: J. B. Lippincott, 1938.

Eckert, Allan W. *The Wilderness War: A Narrative*. Boston: Little, Brown, 1978.

Farb, Peter. *Man's Rise to Civilization: The Cultural Ascent of the Indians of North America*. New York: E. P. Dutton, 1978.

Fenton, William N., ed. *Parker on the Iroquois*. Syracuse: Syracuse UP, 1968.

Fiedel, Stuart J. *Prehistory of the Americas*. Cambridge, England: Cambridge UP, 1987.

Flaherty, Thomas H., ed. *Realm of the Iroquois*. Alexandria, VA: Time-Life Books, 1993.

Gehring, Charles T., and William A. Starma, eds. *A Journey into Mohawk and Oneida Country, 1634-1635: The Journal of Harmen Meyndertsz van den Bogaert*. Syracuse: Syracuse UP, 1988.

George-Kanentiio, Doug. *Iroquois Culture & Commentary*. Santa Fe: Clear Light, 2000.

Graymont, Barbara. *The Iroquois*. New York: Chelsea House, 1988.

—. *The Iroquois in the American Revolution*. Syracuse: Syracuse UP, 1972.

Hale, Horatio, ed. *The Iroquois Book of Rites*. Toronto: U of Toronto P, 1963.

Hall, Charles, H. *The Dutch and the Iroquois*. New York: Francis Hart, 1882.

Hauptman, Lawrence M. *The Iroquois and the New Deal*. Syracuse: Syracuse UP, 1981.

—. *The Iroquois Struggle for Survival: World War II to Red Power*. Syracuse: Syracuse UP, 1986.

Heidt, William, Jr. *O-we-nah: A Legend of Lake Eldridge and 16 Other Iroquois Indian Legends*. Ithaca: DeWitt Historical Society of Tompkins County, 1971.

Henry, Thomas R. *Wilderness Messiah: The Story of Hiawatha and the Iroquois*. New York: William Sloane, 1955.

Hertzberg, Hazel W. *The Great Tree and the Longhouse: The Culture of the Iroquois*. New York: Macmillan, 1966.

Hirschfelder, Arlene, and Pauline Molin. *The Encyclopedia of Native American Religions: An Introduction*. New York: Facts on File, 1992.

Hornung, R. *One Nation under the Gun*. New York: Pantheon Books, 1991.

Hubbard, J. Niles. *Account of Sa-go-ye-wat-ha or Red Jacket*. Albany: Munsell, 1886.

Hunt, G. T. *The Wars of the Iroquois: A Study in Intertribal Trade Relations*. Madison: U of Wisconsin P, 1940.

Jennings, Francis. *The Ambiguous Iroquois Empire*. New York: W. W. Norton, 1984.

—. *The Invasion of America: Indians, Colonialism, and the Cult of Conquest*. New York: W. W. Norton, 1976.

Jennings, Francis, ed. *History and Culture of the Iroquois Diplomacy: An Interdisciplinary Guide to the Treaties of the Six Nations of the Iroquois and their League*. Syracuse: Syracuse UP, 1985.

Johansen, B. E. *Life and Death in Mohawk Country*. Boulder, CO: North American Press, 1993.

Johnson, Elias. *Legends, Traditions, and Laws of the Iroquois or Six Nations and History of the Tuscarora Indians*. Lockport, NY: Union Printing and Publishing, 1881.

Josephy, Alvin M., Jr. *The Indian Heritage of America*. Boston: Houghton Mifflin, 1991.

Kelsay, I. T. *Joseph Brant, 1743-1807: Man of Two Worlds*. Syracuse: Syracuse UP, 1984.

Kimm, S. C. *The Iroquois: A History of the Six Nations of New York*. Middleburgh, NY: Pierre W. Danforth, 1900.

Klees, Emerson. *Legends and Stories of the Finger Lakes Region*. Rochester, NY: Friends of the Finger Lakes Publishing, 1995.

—. *More Legends and Stories of the Finger Lakes Region*. Rochester, NY: Friends of the Finger Lakes Publishing, 1997.

—. *People of the Finger Lakes Region*. Rochester, NY: Friends of the Finger Lakes Publishing, 1995.

Longfellow, Henry Wadsworth. *The Song of Hiawatha*. Chicago: Ferguson, 1968.

Lydekker, John Wolfe. *The Faithful Mohawks*. New York: Macmillan, 1938.

Martin, John H. and Phyllis G. *The Lands of the Painted Post*. Corning, NY: Bookmarks, 1993.

Martin, Paul S., George I. Quimby, and Donald Collier. *Indians before Columbus: Twenty Thousand Years of North American History Revealed by Archaeology*. Chicago: U of Chicago P, 1947.

Mau, Clayton. *The Development of Central and Western New York: From the Arrival of the White Man to the Eve of the Civil War*. N.p.: n.p., 1958.

McCauley, Marlene. *Adventures with a Saint: Kateri Tekakwitha, "Lily of the Mohawks."* Phoenix: Grace House, 1992.

Merrill, Arch. *Land of the Senecas*. New York: American Book-Stratford Press, 1969.

—. *The White Woman and Her Valley*, New York: American Book-Stratford Press, n.d.

Monture, Ethel Brant. *Canadian Portraits: Famous Indians*. Toronto: Clarke, Irwin, 1960.

Morgan, Lewis Henry. *League of the Iroquois*. Secaucus, NJ:
Carol Publishing, 1996.
Moulthrop, Samuel P. *Iroquois*. Rochester, NY: Ernest Hart, 1901.
Myrtle, Minnie (Anna Johnson Miller). *The Iroquois: The Bright Side
of Indian Character*. New York: D. Appleton, 1855.
Noyes, J. O. *The Lakes and Legends of Central New York*. Ovid, NY:
W. E. Morrison, 1857.
Parker, Arthur C. *The Archaeological History of New York*. Albany:
State University of New York, 1922.
—. *The Life of General Ely S. Parker: Last Grand Sachem of the
Iroquois and General Grant's Military Secretary*. Buffalo:
Buffalo Historical Society, 1985.
—. *Seneca Myths and Folk Tales*. Buffalo: Buffalo Historical Society,
1923.
Quain, Buell H. *"The Iroquois." Cooperation and Competition
Among Primitive Peoples*. New York: McGraw-Hill, 1937.
Rapp, Marvin A. *New York State: A Student's Guide to Localized
History*. New York: Teachers College Press, 1968.
Richter, Daniel K. *The Ordeal of the Longhouse*. Chapel Hill:
U of North Carolina P, 1992.
Richter, Daniel K., and James H. Merrill, eds. *Beyond the Covenant
Chain: The Iroquois and Their Neighbors in Indian North
America, 1600-1800*. Syracuse: Syracuse UP, 1887.
Rickard. C. *Fighting Tuscarora: The Autobiography of Chief Clinton
Rickard*. Syracuse: Syracuse UP, 1973.
Ritchie, William A. *The Archaeology of New York State*. Garden City,
NY: Natural History Press, 1969.
—. *Indian History of New York: Part II—The Iroquois Tribes*.
Albany: New York State Museum, n.d.
Ritchie, William A., and Robert E. Funk. *Aboriginal Settlement
Patterns in the Northeast*. Albany: State University of New York,
1973.
Schoolcraft, H. R. *Notes on the Iroquois: Contributions to the
Statistics, Aboriginal History, Antiquities, and General
Ethnology of Western New York*. Albany: Erastus S. Pease, 1847.
Seaver, J. E. *Narrative of the Life of Mary Jemison*. Norman:
U of Oklahoma P, 1992.
Shattuck, G. C. *Oneida Land Claims: A Legal History*. Syracuse:
Syracuse UP, 1991.
Skinner, Charles M. *American Myths and Legends*. Philadelphia:
J. B. Lippincott, 1974.

Smith, Erminnie A. *Myths of the Iroquois*. Washington, DC:
  Smithsonian Institution, 1983.
Snow, Dean R. *The Iroquois*. Cambridge, MA: Blackwell, 1994.
Snow, Dorothy E. *Early Cayuga Days*. King Ferry, NY:
  Genoa Historical Society, 1993.
Speck, Frank Gouldsmith. *The Iroquois*. Bloomfield, MI:
  Cranbrook Institute of Science, 1955.
Starna, W. A. and R. Watkins, eds. *Iroquois Land Claims*. Syracuse:
  Syracuse UP, 1988.
Stephenson, Marion Bailey. *Miracle of the Mohawks*. New York:
  Pageant Press, n.d.
Taft, Grace Ellis. *Cayuga Notes*. Benton Harbor, MI:
  Antiquarian Publishing, 1913.
Tehanetorens (Ray Fadden). *Roots of the Iroquois*. Summertown, TN:
  Native Voices, 2000.
—. *Tales of the Iroquois: Volume I*. Rooseveltown, NY:
  Akwesasne Notes, 1976.
Thompson, Stith, ed. *Tales of the North American Indians*.
  Bloomington: U of Indiana P, 1968.
Trigger, Bruce G. *Handbook of North American Indians—Northeast*.
  Washington, DC: Smithsonian Institution, 1978.
Tuck, J. *Onondaga Iroquois Prehistory: A Study in Settlement
  Archaeology*. Syracuse: Syracuse UP, 1971.
Underhill, Ruth M. *Red Man's America*. Chicago: U of Chicago P.
  1971.
U.S. Census Office. *The Six Nations of New York: The 1892 United
  States Extra Census Bulletin*. Washington, D.C.: Dept. of the
  Interior, Census Office, 1892.
Van Sickle, John. *The Cayuga Indian Reservation and Colonel John
  Harris*. Ithaca, NY: DeWitt Historical Society, 1965.
Vierhile, Robert J. *Nundawao: The Oldest Seneca Village*. Naples,
  NY: Naples Historical Society, 1989.
Waite, D. B. *O-Neh-Da-Te-Car-Ne-O-Di or Up and Down the
  Hemlock*. N.p.: n.p., 1883.
Wallace, Anthony F. C. *The Death and Rebirth of the Seneca*.
  New York: Vintage Books, 1972.
Wallace, Paul A. W. *The White Roots of Peace*. Philadelphia:
  U of Pennsylvania P, 1946.
Wilson, Edmund. *Apologies to the Iroquois*. New York:
  Farrar, Straus and Cudahy, 1960.
Wolfson, Evelyn. *The Iroquois People of the Northeast*.
  Brookfield, CT: Millbrook Press, 1992.

INDEX